MARKUS SÄMMER

Delicious Wintertime

THE COOKBOOK FOR COLD WEATHER ADVENTURES

gestalten

AT HOME

ALPINE HUT BREAKFAST

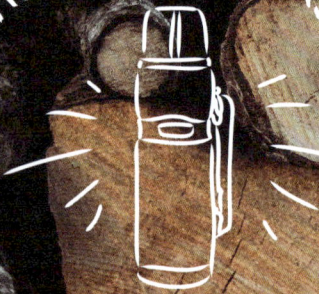

THERMOS FILLERS

WINTER TRAIL SNACKS

HEALTHY ENERGY

PP. 132–171

LONG WINTER EVENINGS

PP. 172–217

WINTRY DESSERTS

PP. 218–241

HOT DRINKS

PP. 242–261

5

AT HOME

ALPINE HUT BREAKFAST

THERMOS FILLERS

WINTER TRAIL SNACKS

HEALTHY ENERGY

LONG WINTER EVENINGS

WINTRY DESSERTS

HOT DRINKS

★ Guide to Recipe Labels

THE LABELS I HAVE ASSIGNED TO EACH RECIPE ARE DESIGNED
TO HELP YOU QUICKLY AND EASILY FIND A RECIPE FOR ANY OCCASION.
THE MEANING OF EACH LABEL IS EXPLAINED BELOW.

★ Wood stove

These dishes are especially well-suited to being prepared in a hut using a real *wood stove*. Of course, you can also prepare them in a regular oven.

★ Deluxe

Recipes labeled *deluxe* signal pure enjoyment and well-being. These recipes will make you especially happy. It's time to spoil yourself!

★ Festive

To find dishes that are part of the special *festive* menu I have created for you for the Christmas holidays, look for this label. Choose your favorites, Happy Holidays, and Season's Greetings!

★ Quick

These are just the right recipes if you are pressed for time and have to be *quick*. A short stop for a packed lunch in the hut, a quick snack with just a few ingredients—these recipes will help you whip up something tasty in no time.

★ Warming

Dishes that warm you inside and out are labeled as *warming*. Especially during the coldest season, and when the weather outside is really foul, they will provide you with comforting warmth.

★ Energy

When your batteries are drained after a long day in the snow, or if you have a long, arduous day outdoors ahead of you, these recipes tick all the right boxes. This label denotes *energy-rich*, delicious dishes that will recharge your batteries and gear you up for the next day's challenges.

★ Vegetarian

This label will quickly help you locate nutritious and flavorful *vegetarian* dishes.

★ Immune booster

Nip that cold in the bud! To stay healthy and fit during the cold, dark season, your body needs plenty of vitamins and special spices. Choose at least two to three of these recipes every week to *boost your immune system*.

★ Slow food

The days are short. Now is the perfect time for genuine *slow food*. Prepare these recipes at a leisurely pace, glass of red wine in hand! These dishes have an extra layer of flavor thanks to their longer preparation time.

★ Winter picnic

The sun is shining, and it's a real winter wonderland out there today. So pack the backpacks, fill the thermoses, load the sled, and head out for a fabulous *winter picnic*. All the recipes you need for an outdoor feast have this label. Of course, they also make a perfect packed lunch for your next backcountry ski tour.

★ Make-ahead

Some dishes always taste better the next day; some taste especially good because they have been allowed to rest overnight. The *make-ahead* label directs you to recipes you can prepare the evening before in a relaxed way, so you can truly enjoy the next day in full.

....

This symbol points the way to small winter hacks—practical and useful tips, tricks, and expert knowledge—that may come in handy during this glorious season.

AT HOME

AT HOME

GOOD THINGS TAKE TIME. NOT EVERY HOLIDAY APARTMENT OR HUT
IS EQUIPPED WITH THE APPLIANCES AND UTENSILS WE TAKE FOR GRANTED AT HOME.
IN THIS SECTION, YOU WILL FIND RECIPES YOU CAN MAKE AHEAD IN THE FALL.
THIS MEANS YOU CAN SAVOR THE BOUNTY OF FALL IN WINTER AND BEYOND.

ORTOVOX
ASCENT 22 AVABAG

PRO ALU 2.7
BIVY
SINGLE
CARBON
FRILUFTS

"Backpack checklist"

WITH THE RIGHT ITEMS IN YOUR BACKPACK YOU WILL ALWAYS BE WELL-PREPARED
AND SAFER IN THE GREAT OUTDOORS, NO MATTER WHAT KIND OF WINTER SPORTS YOU DO.
IF YOU DO HAVE TO GIVE FIRST AID, THE FIRST RULE IN WINTER IS TO ALWAYS PROTECT THE INJURED
FROM HYPOTHERMIA. IT IS FOR THIS REASON THAT YOU SHOULD ALWAYS BRING EXTRA JACKETS,
RESCUE BLANKETS, AND BIVY SACKS, AND DISTRIBUTE THEM AMONG YOUR GROUP.

BASIC EQUIPMENT

No matter what the outdoor activity, always carry
the following items with you in winter:

✗ First-aid kit ✗

✗ Rescue blanket and/or small bivy sack ✗

✗ Thermos flask with hot tea and/or a drinking bottle ✗

✗ A few snacks (see Winter Trail Snacks, pages 108–131) ✗

✗ A warm, small, compressible jacket ✗

✗ Gloves, hat, or headband ✗

✗ Sunscreen ✗

✗ Small headlamp for emergencies (it gets dark quickly in winter) ✗

✗ Fully charged cell phone, protected from the cold ✗

BACKCOUNTRY SKIING/SPLIT BOARDING/
MOUNTAIN SNOWSHOEING

✗ Avalanche airbag, which activates and helps protect you if you are swept up by, or buried in, an avalanche. ✗

✗ Avalanche beacon/transceiver with fully charged batteries (check them beforehand!) ✗

✗ Avalanche shovel and probes ✗

✗ Slope safety card or slope meter (for determining the steepness of a slope and checking the degree of risk) ✗

✗ Map of the area that you are traveling in ✗

✗ Small multi-tool ✗

✗ Change of clothes (such as a dry T-shirt for protection against cooling down too much on the summit) ✗

✗ Lunchbox, well-filled of course. Try the recipes designed for the thermos (pages 78–107) ✗

OPTIONAL

✗ A GPS, a SAM splint (a pliable splint that is so versatile it can be used for many injuries),
a small pair of binoculars, pocketknife, folding cushion, large headlamp ✗

DRIED
wild mushrooms

EACH FALL, SINCE EARLIEST CHILDHOOD,
I HAVE COLLECTED FRESH MUSHROOMS IN THE WOODS.
ALONG WITH FREEZING, DRYING IS A VERY GOOD METHOD
FOR PRESERVING MUSHROOMS, AND HAVING DRIED
MUSHROOMS ON HAND MEANS YOU CAN ENJOY THE FORAGED
TREASURES OF AUTUMN IN WINTER.

STORAGE

Flavorful mushrooms from the *Boletus edulis* family,
such as porcini, orange birch boletes, brown birch boletes,
and rough-stemmed boletes, are especially suitable
for drying. Black trumpet mushrooms, also known as black
chanterelles, are deeply flavorful—though a dried mushroom
mix from your loot can be particularly umami-laden as well.

Vegetarian *Slow food*

PREPERATION

It is important to clean the mushrooms thoroughly. Trim away all the damaged spots and unsightly discolorations (unless you are using boletes, which turn blue when cut or bruised). Thinly slice or shave the mushrooms. Scatter them loosely on baking trays lined with parchment paper. Place the trays in a warm room (such as a furnace room) for 2–3 days. While they are drying, loosen the mushrooms from the parchment and turn gently. If you do not have a warm room, or want to hurry up the process, dry the mushrooms in the oven. Set the convection oven to 120 °F (50 °C). Place the baking trays in the oven and dry the mushrooms for several hours. Stick a cooking spoon in the oven door, or open the oven door now and then, to let the humidity escape while the mushrooms are drying.

When the mushrooms are dry and crispy, allow them to cool completely then transfer them to screw-top jars or airtight containers. Store in a dark, dry, cool place. Properly dried, the mushrooms will keep at least until the next mushroom-hunting season.

Dried mushrooms are an excellent seasoning for sauces, goulashes, and stews. Either add the dried mushrooms to a dish while it cooks (to goulash, for example), or rehydrate the mushrooms by soaking them in water beforehand, then add them to the dish (try this with risotto). If you opt to soak the mushrooms, don't discard the soaking water! Add it to dishes to enhance the flavor.

IMPORTANT

Don't pick mushrooms that you cannot clearly identify. And, even when you do find a spot full of edible mushrooms, please collect them with restraint. Above all, do not pick the old, already soft mushrooms. Harvest mushrooms by cutting the stems horizontally at the ground with a sharp knife, or by gently pulling them from the ground. Use loosely woven baskets for gathering; do not use plastic bags.

Nut-based spreads

NUT-BASED SPREADS, CREAMS, AND BUTTERS ARE QUICK TO MAKE, MUCH HEALTHIER THAN STORE-BOUGHT PRODUCTS, AND HIGHLY VERSATILE. THESE ARE SOME OF THE CHARACTERISTICS OF THE NUT-BASED RECIPES ON THE OPPOSITE PAGE. NOT ONLY DO THEY PROVIDE YOU WITH HEALTHY ENERGY IN WINTER, BUT NUT-BASED SPREADS CONTAIN PLENTY OF VALUABLE MINERALS AND NUTRIENTS AS WELL.

PEANUT BUTTER

MAKES 1 JAR

★ *Vegetarian* ★ *Energy* ★ *Winter Picnic*

*9 OZ (250 G) SHELLED RAW,
UNSALTED PEANUTS
2 TBSP PEANUT OR SUNFLOWER OIL
¼ TSP SALT*

In a dry skillet, toast the nuts and let cool. Transfer to a food processor or blender and process all ingredients until smooth. For a bit of crunch, you can set aside a few pieces of nuts to add afterwards. Transfer the peanut butter to sterilized jars.

SWEET VERSION

1 TBSP HONEY OR AGAVE SYRUP

SPICY VERSION

PINCH OF CHILI PEPPER

SURPRISE VERSION

½ TSP COFFEE BEANS

STORAGE

Stored in the refrigerator, the peanut butter will keep for about 6 weeks.

CASHEW CREAM

MAKES 1 JAR

★ *Vegetarian* ★ *Energy* ★ *Winter picnic*

*9 OZ (250 G) RAW, UNSALTED
CASHEWS
½ ORGANIC LEMON
1 GARLIC CLOVE
2 SOFT PITTED DATES
2–3 TBSP OLIVE OIL
SALT
BLACK PEPPER*

Soak the cashews in water overnight. Drain them in a sieve. Wash, zest, and juice the lemon. Peel the garlic. Using a food processor or blender, process all the ingredients, adding up to ½ glass of water until the desired consistency is achieved. Transfer the cream to sterilized jars.

STORAGE

The cashew cream will keep in the refrigerator for 2–3 weeks.

TRY THIS SPICE-AND-NUT MIXTURE AS A BREADING,
A TOPPING, OR IN SALAD DRESSINGS.
IT LENDS CRUNCH AND A MARVELOUS NUTTY NOTE
TO MANY DIFFERENT DISHES. THIS MEANS YOU ABSOLUTELY
MUST HAVE ONE OR TWO JARS ON HAND.

MAKES 2 JARS

DUKKAH

*1 CUP (125 G) EACH SHELLED RAW WALNUTS,
HAZELNUTS, AND ALMONDS
1 TSP EACH WHOLE CUMIN, CORIANDER,
AND SESAME SEEDS
½ TSP EACH BLACK PEPPERCORNS AND MEDIUM
COARSE SEA SALT OR FLEUR DE SEL*

In a dry skillet, toast the nuts briefly. Coarsely chop the
nuts using a food processor or a knife. In the same skillet,
dry-toast the spices until they release their aroma and
begin to crackle slightly. Let cool, then coarsely grind using
a mortar and pestle. Season with salt. If the salt is very
coarse, grind it briefly with the spices. Mix everything well
and transfer to sterilized jars.

STORAGE

Dukkah keeps for 6–8 weeks.

Pita bread (page 67) is the classic accompaniment for
dukkah, along with a small dipping bowl of quality olive oil.
Try using dukkah as a breading for chicken schnitzel or
vegetables, or go wild and sprinkle it over pork roast after it is
cooked. When you toast the nuts and spices, be careful not to
turn up the heat too high; if they burn they will taste bitter!

1 TSP CUMIN SEEDS

1 TSP CORIANDER SEEDS

1 RED ONION

6–8 GARLIC CLOVES

1 STALK LEMONGRASS

1 IN (2 ½ CM) PIECE OF GALANGAL OR GINGER

3–4 FRESH RED THAI CHILIES

1–2 TBSP CHOPPED CILANTRO ROOT

1 TSP SALT

1 TSP SHRIMP PASTE

ZEST OF 1 ORGANIC LIME

3 TBSP NEUTRAL VEGETABLE OIL, SUCH AS PEANUT OIL

RED CURRY PASTE

MAKES 1 JAR

★ Vegetarian ★ Warming ★ Immune booster

In a dry skillet, toast the cumin and coriander
until fragrant. Finely dice the next 6 ingredients. Using
a mortar and pestle or a blender, blend everything except
the oil into a thick paste. Pour in the oil after processing.

STORAGE

Transfer to a screw-top jar and cover with a thin layer
of oil. The curry paste will keep for several weeks
in the refrigerator.

I LEARNED ABOUT PRESERVED LEMONS ON SURFING TRIPS TO MOROCCO,
WHERE THEY ARE FOUND IN ALMOST EVERY SMALL GROCERY STORE IN LARGE GLASS
JARS. ONE CANNOT IMAGINE MOROCCAN CUISINE WITHOUT THEM. EVEN THOUGH
SOME RECIPES SPECIFY JUST THE LEMON PEEL AND OTHERS JUST THE FLESH, I DON'T
THINK ONE NEEDS TO BE VERY PARTICULAR ABOUT SEPARATING THE TWO. ABOVE ALL,
PRESERVED LEMONS ARE A SERIOUSLY REFRESHING, FLAVORFUL ADDITION TO
MANY MIDDLE EASTERN AND MEDITERRANEAN DISHES. EXPERIMENTS ARE PERMITTED!
THEY ARE PERFECT IN THE CHICKEN TAGINE ON PAGES 162 – 165.

MOROCCAN
preserved lemons

MAKES 2 JARS

14 ORGANIC LEMONS
12 – 14 TSP COARSE SEA SALT
2 BAY LEAVES

It is really important to use pesticide-free organic lemons for this recipe, as the lemons are used whole.
Wash the lemons in hot water and pat dry. Working from top to bottom, make deep lengthwise
cuts in 10 of the 14 lemons, almost cutting them into quarters. Be careful not to completely slice
through the lemons; the quarters should remain attached at the bottom. Gently remove any large seeds.
Juice the remaining 4 lemons.

Press 1 teaspoon of sea salt into each of the cut lemons. Divide the lemons among 2 sterilized jars,
and pack very tightly. Add 1 – 2 tablespoons of sea salt, 1 bay leaf, and half of the lemon juice
to each jar. Slowly pour almost-boiling water into each jar. Watch out that the jars do not crack as you
are filling them! To keep the lemons submerged, place a small sterilized saucer or sterilized stone
directly on the lemons. Seal the jars.

Marinate the lemons for at least 4 – 6 weeks. And remember, every bit of the lemon, not just the peel,
tastes delicious and can be used for cooking. Store the jars on a shelf in your basement or pantry.

STORAGE
Properly stored, the lemons will keep for at least 6 months.

TRADITIONALLY, FISH FILLETS USED FOR PICKLING ARE FROM YOUNG, IMMATURE HERRINGS CAUGHT IN MAY AND JUNE, WHEN THEIR FAT CONTENT IS HIGHEST. AT LEAST ONCE, THOUGH, YOU MUST TRY PICKLING FISH FILLETS FROM FRESHWATER FISH SUCH AS WHITEFISH OR PERCH. FISH CAUGHT IN LOCAL LAKES IS ESPECIALLY SUSTAINABLE. OF COURSE, HERRING, HADDOCK, AND OTHER SMALL, WHITE-FLESHED OCEAN FISH ALSO TASTE DELICIOUS.

ONCE THE FISH IS PICKLED, YOU CAN USE IT IN RECIPES LIKE PICKLED HERRING IN CREAMY SAUCE WITH BOILED POTATOES (PAGE 151). YOU WILL LOVE IT!

PICKLED

Fish fillets

SERVES 4-5

★ Quick   ★ Winter picnic

⅘ CUP (220 G) SALT
10 SKIN-ON FISH FILLETS, DESCALED AND DEBONED
2 CUPS (½ L) WHITE VINEGAR
1 TBSP BLACK PEPPERCORNS
1 TSP ALLSPICE BERRIES
2 TSP JUNIPER BERRIES
2 BAY LEAVES
1 SMALL ONION

First, make the brine. Bring 4 cups (1 l) water and ¾ cup (200 g) salt to a boil. Stir to completely dissolve the salt. Cool the brine well, add the fish fillets, and let marinate for 24 hours in a cold cellar or the refrigerator. Remove the fillets from the brine and briefly rinse under cold water.

Make the pickling liquid. Place 2 cups (½ l) water, the vinegar, the remaining salt, and the spices in a pot. Bring to a boil. Remove the pot from the heat and let cool for 30 minutes. Peel and slice the onion. Arrange the fish fillets in layers in sterilized rubber-seal jars, adding onion slices between each layer. Cover the fish completely with the pickling liquid. Marinate the fish in the refrigerator for a few days before serving.

STORAGE

Properly prepared and refrigerated, the pickled fish will keep for 2 months.

Immune booster *Vegetarian* *Make-ahead*

Homemade Blaukraut
(BRAISED RED CABBAGE)

SERVES 10–12

INGREDIENTS

2 MEDIUM RED CABBAGES

FOR THE MARINADE:
3 ½ OZ (100 G) SUGAR
2 TBSP SALT
FRESHLY GROUND BLACK PEPPER
1 ½ CUPS (350 ML) RED WINE
JUICE OF 2 ORANGES
JUICE OF 2 LEMONS
⅔ CUP (150 ML) APPLE CIDER VINEGAR

FOR THE CABBAGE:
4–5 APPLES
2–3 WHITE ONIONS
4 TBSP SUNFLOWER OIL
OR GOOSE FAT, IF AVAILABLE
(VERY TASTY)
2 TBSP REDCURRANT JELLY
1 SMALL JAR (12 OZ/350 G)
APPLESAUCE
1 SPICE BUNDLE CONTAINING
4 WHOLE CLOVES, 2–3 BAY LEAVES,
1 TBSP CORIANDER SEEDS,
AND 1 TBSP JUNIPER BERRIES
SALT AND PEPPER

PREPERATION

The night before, wash the cabbages and remove the outer leaves. Quarter and core each cabbage. Using a mandoline, knife, or food processor, slice the cabbage very thinly. You may want to use rubber gloves and a plastic cutting board to avoid staining.

Transfer cabbage to a large bowl. Whisk together all the marinade ingredients and pour the marinade over the cabbage. Using your hands, knead the mixture vigorously for about 5 minutes. Cover and place the cabbage in the cellar, pantry, or other cool place to marinate overnight.

The next day, peel, quarter, core, and slice the apples. Peel and dice the onions. Heat the oil or goose fat in a large saucepan. Add the apples and onions, and sauté until the onions are soft and translucent. Add the cabbage and sauté briefly, then add all remaining ingredients. Stirring occasionally, bring the cabbage to a boil over medium heat. Reduce the heat and let simmer for about 30 minutes or until the cabbage is cooked but still has some bite. Season to taste with salt and pepper. Remove the spice bundle and immediately transfer to sterilized jars. A jam funnel will make it easier to fill the jars.

Cover the cabbage with the remaining hot liquid before sealing the jars.

STORAGE

Stored in a cool, dark place, the *blaukraut* will keep for several months. It is a perfect side dish for festive roasts and classic dishes, such as the Roast Pork (pages 181–185).

ZUCCHINI CHUTNEY

MAKES 4 JARS

★ Vegetarian ★ Immune booster ★ Winter picnic

3 – 4 MEDIUM ZUCCHINI
5 ONIONS
6 GARLIC CLOVES
1 IN (2 ½ CM) PIECE OF GINGER
1 CUP (250 ML) WHITE WINE VINEGAR
9 OZ (250 G) BROWN SUGAR
1 TBSP TURMERIC POWDER
1 TBSP CURRY POWDER
1 TBSP HOT HUNGARIAN PAPRIKA
1 TBSP SALT
1 TSP GROUND CINNAMON
1 TSP GROUND CUMIN
HANDFUL OF RAISINS

Wash and finely dice the zucchini. Peel and finely dice the onions, garlic, and ginger. Place all ingredients except the raisins in a pot. Bring to a boil and cook until the zucchini are tender. If desired, you can also use an immersion blender to coarsely purée the mixture. Add the raisins and briefly bring back to a boil. Remove from heat. Using a jam funnel, immediately divide the chutney among 4 sterilized screw-top jars. Seal and store the jars in a cool dark place. Let marinate for at least 4 weeks.

STORAGE

The chutney will keep for up to 1 year, and it tastes wonderful with grilled meat, on crostini, or in sandwiches, among other things.

FIG MUSTARD

MAKES 2 JARS

★ Vegetarian ★ Immune booster ★ Winter picnic

14 OZ (400 G) FRESH FIGS
1 ORGANIC LEMON
7 OZ (200 G) GELLING SUGAR 2:1
2 TBSP LIGHT MUSTARD SEEDS
1 PINCH EACH SALT AND
CAYENNE PEPPER
1 TBSP MUSTARD POWDER

Wash the figs and lemon. Cut the figs into small cubes. Zest and juice the lemon. In a pot, combine the figs and zest with the sugar, mustard seeds, salt, and cayenne pepper. Let macerate for 1 hour, then bring to a brief boil. Reduce the heat and simmer for 3–4 minutes. Add the mustard powder and the lemon juice. Using a jam funnel, immediately transfer the mustard to sterilized screw-top jars. Seal the jars and store in a cool dark place for at least 1 week before using.

STORAGE

The mustard will keep for up to 6 months. It tastes delicious with grilled meat, goat cheese, crostini, or in sandwiches.

TIP If you can't source gelling sugar, use regular sugar and light pectin crystals and follow the package instructions.

IN FALL, IN THE SOUTH, WHEN RIPE FIGS HANG ON THE TREES,
WE OFTEN PREPARE THIS MARVELOUS FRUITY MUSTARD RIGHT ON THE SPOT
IN OUR VW VAN. SINCE THIS MUSTARD IS A REAL MUST-HAVE FOR THE
WINTER PANTRY, IT'S LUCKY THAT FIGS CAN BE PURCHASED AT THE PEAK
OF FRESHNESS EVEN IN MORE NORTHERN CLIMES. WE LOVE THIS MUSTARD
SERVED WITH SARDINIAN PECORINO CHEESE AND A CRUSTY BAGUETTE.

Energy   *Winter picnic*

ELISEN GERMAN
Gingerbread Cookies

MAKES 10 COOKIES

INGREDIENTS

FOR THE COOKIES:
5 ORGANIC EGGS
¼ TSP SALT
14 OZ (400 G) DARK CANE SUGAR
3 ½ OZ (100 G) EACH FINELY CHOPPED ORGANIC CANDIED
ORANGE AND LEMON PEEL
7 OZ (200 G) EACH GROUND RAW ALMONDS AND HAZELNUTS
3 ½ OZ (100 G) EACH CHOPPED RAW ALMONDS AND HAZELNUTS
1–2 TBSP GERMAN GINGERBREAD SPICE MIX (IN SPECIALTY STORES OR ONLINE)
LARGE OBLATEN WAFERS, IF AVAILABLE

FOR THE GLAZE:
9 OZ (250 G) DARK CHOCOLATE COUVERTURE
1 TBSP COCONUT OIL

PREPERATION

Make the cookie dough the night before. Whisk the eggs together with the salt until stiff peaks form. Still whisking, gradually add in the sugar. Add all remaining ingredients except the wafers, and stir to combine. Cover the bowl and refrigerate overnight.

The next day, preheat the oven to 300 °F (150 °C). Line a baking tray with parchment paper. Using a spoon, spread ½-inch (1 ¼ cm) of dough on top of each wafer, smoothing it to the wafer edges. Arrange the cookies on the baking tray. (If you can't get oblaten wafers, spread the dough directly on the parchment paper.) Bake for 30–35 minutes. Remove from the oven and let cool.

To make the glaze, melt the chocolate and coconut oil in a double boiler, stirring often. Brush the glaze over the top of the cookies, and set cookies on a wire rack in a cool place. When completely cool, layer cookies loosely in airtight containers, using parchment paper between the layers if needed.

STORAGE

Stored in a cool place in an airtight container, the cookies should keep for at least 4 weeks.

Cookie baking mixes

HERE ARE SOME GREAT COOKIE MIXES I HAVE PUT TOGETHER
FOR DAYS WHEN YOU ARE COMPLETELY SNOWED IN. THEY CAN EASILY
BE MADE AHEAD AT HOME AND TAKEN ALONG TO A MOUNTAIN CABIN
OR ON YOUR WINTER HOLIDAY. BY ADDING JUST ONE OR TWO
WET INGREDIENTS, YOU CAN SERVE OVEN-FRESH COOKIES IN A FLASH
ANY TIME. OR, YOU CAN PLACE THE COOKIE MIXES IN JARS AT HOME
AND STORE THEM IN THE PANTRY. ATTRACTIVELY PACKAGED,
THE MIXES ALSO MAKE A UNIQUE GIFT.

MAKES 1 JAR OF EACH

Stored in airtight containers in a cool dark place,
the cookies should keep for at least 4 weeks.

★ *Energy* ★ *Winter picnic* ★ *Festive*

CHRISTMAS STOLLEN BALLS

5 ½ OZ (150 G) ALL-PURPOSE FLOUR
1 TSP ACTIVE DRY YEAST
1 ¾ OZ (50 G) DARK CANE SUGAR
2 TBSP ORGANIC CANDIED ORANGE PEEL, FINELY CHOPPED
2 TBSP ORGANIC CANDIED LEMON PEEL, FINELY CHOPPED
1 ¾ OZ (50 G) RAW GROUND ALMONDS
1 ¾ OZ (50 G) RAW CHOPPED ALMONDS
2 TBSP VANILLA SUGAR (FOR HOMEMADE
VANILLA SUGAR SEE TIP, PAGE 43)
1 TBSP STOLLEN SPICE MIX (GROUND CARDAMOM, ALLSPICE,
CINNAMON, CLOVES, AND MACE; IN SPECIALTY STORES OR ONLINE)
PINCH OF SALT

WET INGREDIENTS:
½ CUP (100 ML) WARM MILK
1 ¾ OZ (50 G) SOFTENED BUTTER

MELTED BUTTER (OPTIONAL)
POWDERED SUGAR (OPTIONAL)

Place all dry ingredients in a mixing bowl. Add the wet
ingredients and knead to make a smooth, elastic dough. Cover and
let rise in a warm place for 1 hour. Preheat the oven to 360 °F (180 °C).
Line a baking tray with parchment paper. Moisten your hands
and shape the dough into bite-sized balls. Arrange the cookies
on the baking tray and bake for about 20 minutes.

If desired, brush the cookies with a bit of melted butter
and dust with powdered sugar.

VANILLA CRESCENT COOKIES WITH MATCHA

★ Energy ★ Winter picnic ★ Festive

3 ½ OZ (100 G) ALL-PURPOSE FLOUR
1 ¾ OZ (50 G) GROUND RAW ALMONDS
1 ¾ OZ (50 G) GROUND RAW WALNUTS
½ TSP BAKING POWDER
2 ⅓ OZ (65 G) DARK CANE SUGAR
1 TSP GROUND VANILLA (OR MAKE
IT YOURSELF BY GRINDING A DRIED
VANILLA BEAN)
1 TSP MATCHA POWDER
PINCH OF SALT

WET INGREDIENTS:
1 EGG
2 OZ (60 G) SOFTENED BUTTER

VANILLA SUGAR AND MATCHA POWDER,
FOR ROLLING (OPTIONAL)

Place all dry ingredients in a mixing bowl. Add the wet ingredients and knead to make a smooth, elastic dough. Shape the dough into ½-inch (1 ¼ cm) wide logs, then slice into 1-inch (2 ½ cm) pieces. Roll each piece between the palms of your hands to form pointed ends, then gently shape into crescents. Preheat the oven to 360 °F (180 °C). Place the cookies on a baking tray lined with parchment and bake for 8–10 minutes.

If desired, roll the cookies in a mixture of vanilla sugar and matcha powder while still warm.

SPEKULATIUS SPICE COOKIES

★ Energy ★ Winter picnic ★ Festive

5 ½ OZ (150 G) ALL-PURPOSE FLOUR
3 ½ OZ (100 G) GROUND RAW ALMONDS
1 TSP BAKING POWDER
3 ½ OZ (100 G) DARK CANE SUGAR
1 ¾ OZ (50 G) CHOCOLATE CHIPS
2 TBSP VANILLA SUGAR (FOR HOMEMADE
VANILLA SUGAR SEE TIP, PAGE 43)
½ TSP EACH GROUND CINNAMON, GROUND
CARDAMOM, GROUND GINGER, GROUND MACE
¼ TSP GROUND BLACK PEPPER
PINCH OF GROUND CLOVES
PINCH OF SALT

WET INGREDIENTS:
1 EGG
4 ½ OZ (125 G) SOFTENED BUTTER

Place all dry ingredients in a mixing bowl. Add the wet ingredients and knead to make a smooth, elastic dough. Preheat the oven to 360 °F (180 °C) and line a baking tray with parchment paper. Moisten a teaspoon and portion the dough, then arrange the cookies on the baking tray. Bake for 12–15 minutes.

Spice mixes and syrups

MAKES 2 BOTTLES OF EACH

THE AROMA OF WINTER AND THE HOLIDAY SEASON WILL WAFT THROUGH
THE KITCHEN AS YOU MAKE THESE SPICE MIXES AND SYRUPS. AS A RULE, ALWAYS
COMBINE THE LIQUIDS AND SUGAR IN A POT FIRST, BRING TO A BOIL, THEN ADD
THE REMAINING INGREDIENTS. FOR MORE INTENSE FLAVOR, LET THE SYRUPS STEEP
FOR A FEW HOURS OR OVERNIGHT IN A COOL PLACE BEFORE STRAINING THEM
THROUGH A FINE-MESH SIEVE AND TRANSFERRING THEM TO STERILIZED BOTTLES.

TO PROLONG THEIR SHELF LIFE, AFTER STRAINING THE SYRUPS PLACE THEM
IN A POT AND BOIL BRIEFLY. TRANSFER TO STERILIZED BOTTLES WHILE STILL HOT.
TO FURTHER EXTEND THE SHELF LIFE, ADD A BIT OF ASCORBIC ACID (VITAMIN C)
OR CITRIC ACID; USE 2 TBSP ACID PER 4 CUPS (1 L) LIQUID.

Quick *Winter picnic*

BAKED APPLE SYRUP

3 CUPS (750 ML) APPLE JUICE   2.2 LB (1 KG) BROWN SUGAR
4 CINNAMON STICKS   1 VANILLA BEAN   1 STAR ANISE   2 DROPS ALMOND EXTRACT

Quick *Immune booster* *Winter picnic*

GINGER ORANGE SYRUP

4 CUPS (1 L) WATER   1 LB 2 OZ (500 G) SUGAR
10 OZ (300 G) PEELED FRESH GINGER   ½ TSP GROUND TURMERIC
4 ALLSPICE BERRIES OR PEPPERCORNS   4 ORGANIC ORANGES

Wash, zest, and juice the oranges.
Cover and let simmer for 10 minutes.

Quick *Winter picnic*

HAZELNUT SYRUP

2 CUPS (500 ML) WATER   1LB 2 OZ (500 G) BROWN SUGAR
7 OZ (200 G) RAW HAZELNUTS

In a dry skillet, toast the hazelnuts until fragrant. Remove from heat and chop.
Return to skillet, add the sugar, and cook until it starts to caramelize. Add water to deglaze.
Boil over medium heat for about 10 minutes.

You can use the syrups to concoct hot wintry drinks in no time, to refine desserts, or to sweeten teas.

Quick *Warming*

MULLED WINE SPICES

3 TBSP CANDIED BROWN SUGAR   6 WHOLE CLOVES
2 – 3 CARDAMOM PODS   2 CINNAMON STICKS   1 STAR ANISE
DRIED ORANGE PEEL (YOU CAN ALSO MAKE THIS YOURSELF)

HOMEMADE
Liqueurs

THE ABILITY TO SAVOR THE FRUITY BOUNTY OF AUTUMN IN WINTER
DEFINITELY IMPROVES ONE'S MOOD! BERRIES AND FRUIT FREEZE WELL, OF COURSE,
BUT MAKE SURE SOME FRESH BERRIES ALSO FIND THEIR WAY INTO YOUR LIQUEUR
BOTTLES. ENJOYING THESE FLAVORFUL LIQUEURS DURING THE COLDEST
TIME OF YEAR WILL WARM YOUR BODY AND SOUL.

MAKES 1 BOTTLE OF EACH

★ *Quick* ★ *Festive*

PLUM LIQUEUR

14 OZ (400 G) RIPE PLUMS
¾ CUP (150 G) BROWN ROCK SUGAR CRYSTALS
1 CINNAMON STICK
1 PIECE ORGANIC ORANGE PEEL
2–3 WHOLE CLOVES
2 ¾ CUPS (700 ML) BROWN OR WHITE RUM

Wash, pit, and halve the plums. Put them in a large, wide-bellied bottle or a large preserving jar.
Add the sugar and spices, then pour in the rum.

Let steep for at least 4 weeks in a cool cellar, pantry, or other cool and dark place.
Strain through a sieve and transfer to sterilized bottles.
Reserve the plums to serve either in liqueurs or as a boozy companion for wintry desserts (page 218 onwards).

★ *Quick*

EGG LIQUEUR

8 ORGANIC EGG YOLKS
9 OZ (250 G) POWDERED SUGAR
11 FL OZ (340 G) SWEETENED
CONDENSED MILK
1 CUP (250 ML) BRANDY
OR WHITE RUM
1 TONKA BEAN, GRATED (OR THE
SEEDS OF ½ VANILLA BEAN)

VARIATION

COCONUT EGG LIQUEUR:
REPLACE THE CONDENSED MILK
WITH COCONUT MILK

In a metal bowl, whisk together the egg yolks and sugar. Slowly stir in the condensed milk and the brandy or rum. Add the grated tonka bean or vanilla seeds.

Place the bowl over a pan of barely simmering hot water. Whisk constantly and slowly until thick and foamy.

TIP The "rose test": When you think the liqueur is thick enough, dip a wooden cooking spoon into it. Gently blow on the back of the spoon. If rose-like petals form, the consistency and temperature (which is important when using raw egg yolks) are perfect. Do not cook the eggs for too long or they will curdle.

Using a funnel, transfer the egg liqueur to sterilized bottles. Stored in the refrigerator, it will keep for up to 4 weeks.

Quick

BLACKCURRANT LIQUEUR

Wash the blackcurrants and pluck out any stems. Place the blackcurrants in a sterilized wide-bellied bottle or a large preserving jar. Peel and slice the ginger. Split the vanilla bean and scrape out the seeds. Place the ginger, vanilla seeds, and sugar crystals in the bottle or jar, then pour in the rum or vodka.

Steep the blackcurrant liqueur for at least 4 weeks in a cool cellar, pantry, or other cool and dark place. Strain the liqueur through a sieve and transfer to sterilized bottles. Reserve the strained berries to spoon over vanilla or walnut ice cream, or as a boozy companion for wintry desserts (page 218 onwards).

Blackcurrant liqueur tastes good on its own, in long drinks, or in cocktails like Kir—where it is topped with sparkling wine or prosecco—and Kir Royal, made with champagne (which, in my opinion, makes the champagne lose its special nutty flavor).

1 LB 2 OZ (500 G) BLACKCURRANTS
1 SMALL PIECE OF GINGER
½ VANILLA BEAN
9 OZ (250 G) BROWN ROCK
SUGAR CRYSTALS
2 ¾ CUPS (700 ML) WHITE RUM
OR VODKA

TIP When a recipe calls for vanilla seeds, don't throw away the pods! Place them in a screw-top jar together with some sugar and shake. After about a week, you will have wonderful, homemade vanilla sugar on hand.

ALPINE HUT BREAKFAST

ALPINE HUT BREAKFAST

FOR ME, HOMEMADE BREAKFAST IN A COZY HUT
IS THE OPTIMAL WAY TO KICK-START AN ACTIVE
DAY IN THE MOUNTAINS. THE EARLY BIRDS LIGHT THE FIRST
FIRE AND GET A POT OF COFFEE GOING. THE CRACKLING
OF THE FIRE AND THE WAFTING AROMA OF COFFEE LURE EVEN
THE LATE RISERS OUT FROM UNDER THE COVERS.
AND JUST LIKE THAT, BREAKFAST BECOMES A TEAM EFFORT.

EXPEDITION TO THE WESTERN ALPS

Porridge

ORIGINALLY FROM SCOTLAND, WARM
OATMEAL PORRIDGE WAS ONCE CONSIDERED
BORING AT BEST. BUT IT IS NOW BACK IN
VOGUE, AND FOR GOOD REASON: PORRIDGE
IS HIGHLY VERSATILE AND IT CAN BE
PREPARED IN SO MANY DELICIOUS WAYS,
NOT TO MENTION THE BENEFITS OF ITS
RELATIVELY HIGH CARBOHYDRATE AND FLUID
CONTENT FOR FUELING AN ACTIVE DAY.

SERVES 2

SPICED PORRIDGE
WITH DATES AND WINTER APPLE

★ Quick ★ Immune booster ★ Energy

1 WINTER APPLE
1 CUP QUICK OATS
1 CUP DAIRY MILK, ALMOND MILK,
OR OAT MILK
½ TBSP CANE SUGAR
¼ TSP CINNAMON
2 – 3 CARDAMOM PODS
4 TBSP RAISINS
2 TBSP PITTED AND COARSELY
CHOPPED DATES
2 TBSP COARSELY CHOPPED WALNUTS
2 TSP HONEY

Wash, core, and dice the apple. In a saucepan combine the oats, milk, sugar, cinnamon, and cardamom. Add 1 cup water and bring to a boil. Add the raisins and apple. Lower heat and simmer, stirring constantly, until the porridge is thick and creamy. Remove the cardamom pods and divide the porridge between 2 bowls. Sprinkle with the dates and walnuts; drizzle with the honey.

FRUITY
FITNESS PORRIDGE
WITH POMEGRANATE AND FIGS

★ Quick ★ Immune booster ★ Energy

1 CUP DAIRY MILK, ALMOND MILK,
OR OAT MILK
PINCH OF TURMERIC
½ TBSP CANE SUGAR
1 CUP QUICK OATS
½ PEAR
1 RIPE POMEGRANATE
4 FIGS (IDEALLY FRESH,
OTHERWISE DRIED)
4 TBSP PECANS
2 TBSP MAPLE SYRUP

In a saucepan combine the milk, turmeric, and sugar. Add 1 cup water and bring to a boil. Sprinkle in the oats. Reduce heat and simmer, stirring constantly, until the porridge is thick and creamy. Wash, core, and dice the pear. Halve the pomegranate and remove the seeds: hold each half, cut-side down, over a bowl. Whack the pomegranate skin with a spoon until all the seeds fall out. Cut the figs into quarters. Just before serving, stir the pomegranate seeds and pear into the porridge. Divide the porridge among 2 deep bowls, decorate with the figs and pecans, and drizzle with the maple syrup.

★ Make-ahead ★ Energy ★ Slow food

ORIGINAL
Swiss Bircher muesli

SERVES 2

THIS IS A TRUE MUESLI CLASSIC THAT TASTES REALLY GOOD,
ESPECIALLY IN WINTER. A SWISS ENERGY BOMB, IT KEEPS YOU FEELING
FULL FOR QUITE A LONG TIME AND POWERS YOU
UP FOR AN ACTIVE DAY IN WINTER.

INGEDIENTS

1 HEAPING CUP (ABOUT 100 G) QUICK OATS
2 TBSP RAISINS
1 ¼ CUPS (300 ML) DAIRY MILK, ALMOND MILK, OR OAT MILK
2 APPLES
1 TBSP HONEY
2 TBSP CHOPPED HAZELNUTS

PREPERATION

The night before, place the oats, raisins, and milk in a bowl.
Stir, cover, and let the oats soak overnight in the refrigerator.
The next day, before serving, wash, core, and finely grate
the apples (peeled or unpeeled). Stir them into the muesli along
with the honey and hazelnuts.

To jazz up the muesli, add some plain yogurt, walnuts,
and a sprinkle of cinnamon.

EGG-AND-HAM
TOAST CUPS

4 SLICES WHOLE WHEAT BREAD
2 TSP BUTTER
4 SLICES HAM, SMOKED BACON,
OR SMOKED SALMON
4 EGGS
SALT AND BLACK PEPPER
2 TBSP GRATED GRUYÈRE
CHEESE
½ BUNCH CHIVES, CHOPPED, OR
2 TSP MICROGREENS

Preheat the oven to 360 °F (180 °C). Stack the slices of bread and trim the crusts. Using a wooden rolling pin or a wine bottle, slightly flatten each slice of bread. Lightly butter each bread slice on both sides. Press each slice into a muffin tin or small ramekin to make a toast "cup." Top each toast cup with a slice of ham, bacon, or salmon. Crack 1 egg over each toast cup, being careful not to break the yolk. Season lightly with salt and pepper, then sprinkle with Gruyère. Bake for about 15 minutes. Serve hot, garnished with chives or microgreens.

VEGETARIAN VERSION

You can replace the ham, bacon, or salmon with long, thin slices of zucchini.

BAKED
BANANA ROLLS

A VERITABLE ALL-IN-ONE BREAKFAST DISH, THESE BANANA ROLLS GIVE YOU EVERYTHING YOU NEED TO START THE DAY WELL. AND THEY ARE SO SCRUMPTIOUS THAT THEY CAN EASILY DOUBLE AS DESSERT: JUST ADD A SCOOP OF ICE CREAM.

4 SLICES WHOLE WHEAT BREAD
1 BANANA
2 EGGS
4 TBSP MILK
2 TBSP CINNAMON SUGAR, PLUS
EXTRA FOR SERVING (TO MAKE IT,
COMBINE ¼ CUP SUGAR AND
1 TBSP CINNAMON, THEN STORE
IN AN AIRTIGHT CONTAINER)
2 TBSP FRESH CHEESE, SUCH
AS RICOTTA (OR CHOCOLATE SPREAD,
FOR A CHOCOLATE VARIATION)
2 – 3 TBSP COCONUT OIL OR
VEGETABLE OIL

Stack the slices of bread and trim the crusts. Using a rolling pin or a wine bottle, lightly flatten each slice. Peel and quarter the banana (cut it in half crosswise, then cut each half down the middle lengthwise). If needed, cut the banana quarters to the same length as the bread slices. In a deep plate, whisk together the eggs, milk, and cinnamon sugar. Spread cheese (or chocolate spread) on each slice of bread. Place a banana slice along the edge, roll up each slice, then dip it in the egg mixture. In a non-stick skillet, heat the oil. Fry the rolls on all sides until golden brown. Sprinkle with a pinch of cinnamon sugar and serve.

MAKES 2 SERVINGS

Sporty breakfasts

Egg whites are packed with nutrition. A vital
component of a balanced diet, they are
an important building block for muscles,
and especially important for sporty,
active people.

Chicken eggs are a good—and delicious—source
of protein. Growing up, we kept a few happy
chickens at home, so I know firsthand the difference the
welfare of the chickens can make. I strongly recommend
using only free-range, organic eggs from
small local producers. Happy chickens make
better-tasting, healthier food.

BAKED AVOCADOS

Quick ★ *Energy* ★ *Wood stove*

1 AVOCADO
1 SMALL TOMATO
2 EGGS
½ BUNCH CHIVES, CHOPPED
SALT AND BLACK PEPPER
½ LEMON

OPTIONAL:
SRIRACHA SAUCE

Preheat the oven to 400 °F (200 °C). Cut the avocado in half and remove the pit. Quarter, seed, and finely dice the tomato, then fill the avocado halves with it. Separate the eggs. Carefully top each avocado half with 1 wholeegg. Whisk the egg whites with the chives and season with salt and pepper. Spoon egg white mixture over each avocado half. Place in a heatproof baking dish. Bake for 15 minutes.

To serve, drizzle the avocados with a bit of lemon juice and sriracha sauce, if using. Serve with dark wholegrain bread.

SWEET POTATO FRITTATA
WITH KALE

★ *Energy* ★ *Immune booster*

1 SMALL RED ONION
4 EGGS
½ CUP MILK
SALT AND BLACK PEPPER
1 SMALL SWEET POTATO
2 KALE LEAVES
2 TBSP SUNFLOWER OIL
3 ½ OZ (100 G) FETA CHEESE

OPTIONAL:
1 TBSP PINE NUTS

Peel and very thinly slice the onion. Beat the eggs with the milk; season with salt and pepper. Peel and coarsely grate the sweet potato. Wash the kale, remove the ribs, and chop the leaves. Heat the oil in a large non-stick sauté pan. Add the vegetables and the pine nuts, if using, and sauté briefly. Pour the egg mixture into the pan, then coarsely crumble the feta cheese over the top. Cook over medium heat until golden brown underneath and just barely set on top. Invert frittata onto a large plate, then return to pan and cook the other side until golden brown. Slide the frittata onto a cutting board, slice it into quarters, and serve.

★ Wood stove   ★ Winter picnic

Crusty farmer's bread

HEARTY FARMER'S BREAD IS A MUST-HAVE FOR BREAKFAST OR A GOOD
PICNIC. IT IS TRADITIONALLY BAKED IN THE OVEN, IDEALLY ON A BAKING STONE,
BUT TRY BAKING IT IN AN OLD ENAMELED POT, TOO. THE BREAD KEEPS A LONG TIME
BAKED THIS WAY, AND IT ALSO LOOKS REALLY ATTRACTIVE, MAKING IT A
NICE HOMEMADE GIFT FOR LOVED ONES AND FRIENDS. DON'T BE AFRAID
TO BAKE BREAD—THIS ONE ALWAYS TURNS OUT WELL!

INGREDIENTS

0.75 OZ (21 G) FRESH YEAST OR
2 TSP ACTIVE DRY YEAST   1 TBSP HONEY
9 OZ (250 G) ALL-PURPOSE FLOUR
½ CUP (125 ML) BUTTERMILK
1 TSP DIASTATIC MALT POWDER (ONLINE
OR AT BREWING SUPPLY STORES)
9 OZ (250 G) SPELT FLOUR   1 TSP BREAD
SPICE MIX (FENNEL, CORIANDER,
ALLSPICE, AND CARAWAY; SEE RIGHT)
2 TSP SALT   1 TBSP FRUIT VINEGAR

PREPERATION

BREAD SPICE MIX:

In a dry skillet, toast equal amounts of fennel
seeds, coriander seeds, allspice berries,
and caraway seeds, then crush finely using
a mortar and pestle.

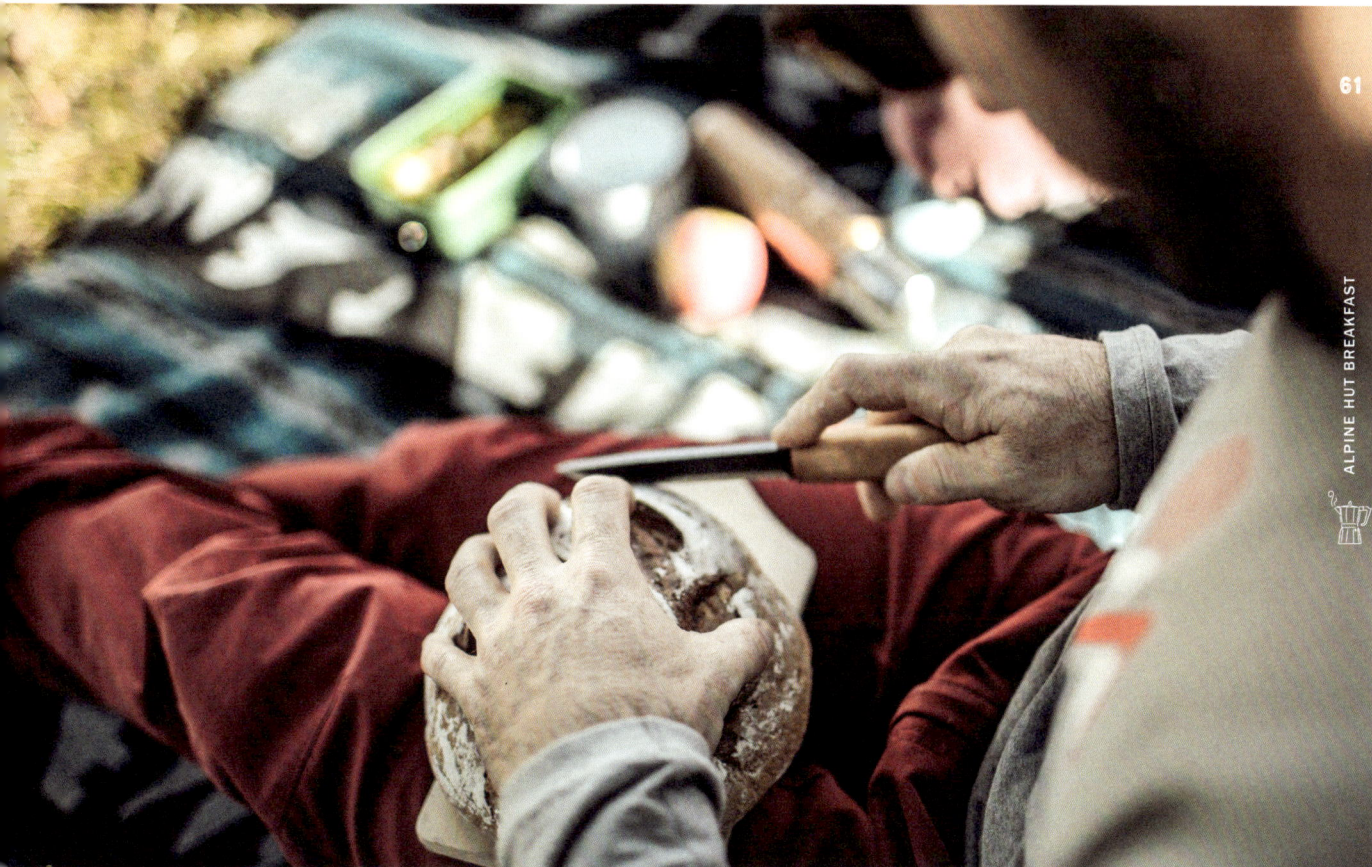

Make a starter: Warm ½ cup (125 ml) water in a small saucepan. Add the yeast and honey, and stir until completely dissolved. Sprinkle in half of the all-purpose flour and stir to combine. Place the mixture in a large bowl. Cover the bowl and leave it in a warm place for 10–15 minutes or until little bubbles form.

Mix the dough: Warm the buttermilk slightly. To the starter gradually add the buttermilk, the remaining all-purpose flour, and the malt powder. Work in all the remaining ingredients and knead for about 10 minutes, until the dough is smooth and elastic and no longer sticks to the edge of the bowl. Work in a bit more flour or water as needed.

Shape the dough into a ball and place it in a bowl lightly dusted with flour. Cover the bowl and let the dough rise in a warm place for about 1 hour. Transfer the dough to a lightly floured work surface, stretch it out, and fold it back together. Stretch and fold 5 to 10 times.

Lightly brush a heavy cast iron pot, enameled pot, or a roasting pan with oil, then dust with a thin layer of flour. Reshape the dough into a ball and place it in the middle of the pot. Brush the top of the dough with a bit of water. Using a knife, cut a cross shape into the top of the dough. Sift a bit of flour over the top of the dough and cover the pot with a lid. Place the pot or pan in a cold oven. Heat the oven to 475 °F (240 °C) or fire up the wood stove.

Bake for 1 hour. Cool the loaf briefly on a wire rack. For a softer crust, wrap the bread in a kitchen towel as it cools.

TIP

Of course you can also bake the bread the traditional way, without using a pot. Put a baking stone or baking tray on the lowest oven rack, and place a small heatproof bowl filled with water on the rack. Preheat the oven to 425 °F (220 °C). After shaping the dough into a ball, cover the bowl. Leave the dough to rise as above, adding 30 minutes to the rising time (90 minutes in total). Brush the top of the dough with a bit of water. Using a knife, cut a cross shape into the top of the dough. Sift a bit of flour over the top of the dough. Using a peel, transfer the dough onto the baking stone or baking tray in the oven.

After about 20 minutes, reduce the oven temperature to 360 °F (180 °C) or stop adding wood to the stove. Bake the bread for 1 hour.

EXPEDITION TO THE WESTERN ALPS

TRAVERSING THE DAUPHINÉ ON SKIS

DUE TO THEIR WILD, CRAGGY RIDGES, AND SECLUDED, INACCESSIBLE WILDERNESS, THE DAUPHINÉ ALPS ARE ALSO KNOWN AS THE KARAKORUM OF THE ALPS. IN SUMMER THEY ARE A DREAM GOAL FOR EXTREME CLIMBERS WHO WANT TO WIN THEIR WESTERN ALP SPURS. OUR GOAL WAS TO ATTEMPT AN EXTREMELY DEMANDING AND SECLUDED FIVE-DAY BACKCOUNTRY SKI TOUR OF THE AREA. OUR STARTING POINT WAS LA GRAVE, THE WORLD-FAMOUS FREERIDE AND EXTREME-SKI MECCA.

From La Grave (4848 ft / 1481 m) we ride the antiquated
gondola up toward the La Meije summit, to reach
our starting point at 10564 ft / 3220 m. Our climb over
the Glacier de la Girose, passing threatening seracs,
brings us to Col de la Girose (11541 ft / 3518 m).
Once we arrive at the very steep entrance to the couloir,
it slowly dawns on us how demanding the expedition
that lies ahead will be from this point on. After a short
abseil through the couloir entrance with our skis on,
we ski down through the cannon barrel without a rope.
The chute is at least 45 degrees steep, but still
relatively good for skiing down. Once we reach the
neighboring valley, we climb up to Brèche du Rateâu
(10679 ft / 3255 m) using ice axes and crampons. Again,
it is very steep...but now comes wonderful downhill
skiing from a 3280 ft / 1000 m altitude. Then, we carry
our skis along a snow-free summer path to the small
mountain climbing village of La Bérarde 5613 ft
(1711 m), which is almost completely isolated in winter.

DAY 2

Baked polenta and braised beef stew in the evening, an
ample breakfast in the morning: the delicious food in our
hostel has energized us. And, the only shower of the
entire trip was here—with hot water, no less. After
saying our goodbyes, and in an excellent mood, we
go up at a leisurely pace to the Refuge de Temple-Écrins
(7906 ft / 2410 m). A cold and secluded winter room
awaits us here, in a mountain hut that is unmanaged
in winter. For this part of the tour we had to stow
food for five, two portable gas stoves, and gas canisters
in our backpacks. The menu is simple and nutritious.
We had packed all the ingredients separately into small
bags to reduce the weight.

DAY 3

A hard crust has formed overnight. Today, the chance
of warming during the day is too high for us to risk,
so we start off very early, at first light. Because of the
steep slopes and the danger of slides along parts of the
route, we carry our skis. Climbing easily, using crampons
and ice axes, we make our way up to the Col de la
Temple (10898 ft / 3322 m). Disappointingly, the south
chute we had planned to ski down was mostly snow-free.
This means we have to negotiate tricky spots with many
loose boulders without a rope. We do all this wearing

ski boots and carrying our skis on our backpacks! And, the climbing difficulty is in the high end of grade 4, so it isn't exactly trivial. If we slip, it's 984 ft/300 m down—definitely not for the faint of heart. Once we reach the Glacier Noir we ski down fabulous slopes to the Refuge Cézanne (6148 ft/1874 m). Here, it's time to get the ski skins on again and climb up to the Refuge du Glacier Blanc (8366 ft/2550 m). The total climb was 5249 ft/1600 m in altitude. The longest leg of our ski tour is accomplished.

We have to abandon our planned route to the summit of the Dôme de Neige des Écrins (13173 ft/4015 m). We pass the Refuge des Écrins on a gigantic glacier basin. Due to the high-altitude storm, with winds of up to 62 mph (100 km/h), we opt for a smaller peak on the more leeward side. Then we go back to the Refuge des Écrins, where we watch a breathtaking sunset that bathes the Dôme in a fiery red light and fills us with an overwhelming sense of gratitude.

DAY 5

From the Refuge des Écrins we head to the most demanding crux: traversing the Col Émile Pic. This had already caused us many headaches during the planning phase. One of the pitches here goes up a near-vertical rock face, and requires mixed climbing with ice axes and crampons. Given the adverse and still very stormy conditions, even our party's strongest climber, who is leading the pitch, has a hard time reaching the anchor point. But the path is clear now; thanks to him, we are well-secured and able to overcome this last hurdle. Now we ski down the steep hanging glacier, the Glacier de la Plate des Agneaux (7546 ft/2300 m), an exhilarating finale with very athletic skiing all the way down and into the valley. Soon we're carrying our skis again, and we walk for an hour to Villar-d'Arêne (5413 ft/1650 m).

Pita bread

WITH SESAME AND NIGELLA

THE WONDERFUL SMELL OF FRESHLY BAKED BREAD ENTICES ALL THE SLEEPYHEADS OUT FROM UNDER THEIR BLANKETS. THIS PITA BREAD COMES TOGETHER EASILY AND IS DELICIOUSLY FLAVORFUL. TOPPED WITH SANDWICH FIXINGS, IT ALSO PACKS WELL FOR TAKING ALONG IN YOUR BACKPACK WHEN THE OUTDOORS CALLS.

2 TSP ACTIVE DRY YEAST OR
21 G (0.75 OZ) FRESH YEAST
1 TSP SUGAR
9 OZ (250 G) SPELT FLOUR OR WHOLE
WHEAT FLOUR
½ TSP SALT
1 TSP OLIVE OIL
1 EGG
1 TBSP MILK OR WATER
1 TSP NIGELLA SEEDS
1 TSP SESAME SEEDS

Place the yeast, sugar, and a bit of warm water in a cup. Stir to combine, and let the mixture ferment briefly. Place the flour, salt, yeast mixture, and oil in a bowl. Gradually add about ½ cup (125 ml) warm water, kneading the dough until it is smooth and elastic. Cover the bowl and let the dough rise in a warm place for 30–45 minutes.

Knead the dough again briefly and transfer to a floured work surface. Using a rolling pin (or a wine bottle, in a pinch) roll out a flat piece of dough a bit larger than the size of your palm. Beat the egg together with 1 tablespoon of milk or water and brush it over the dough. With the tips of your fingers, poke the dough a few times. Scatter nigella and sesame seeds on top. Let the dough rise for another 20 minutes. While the dough is rising, preheat the oven to 480 °F (250 °C). Place a baking stone in the oven or line a baking tray with parchment paper. Bake for about 8 minutes or until light golden brown.

COLD-PROOFED

Buns

THE AROMA OF FRESHLY BAKED BUNS FIRST THING IN THE MORNING IS NOTHING SHORT OF HEAVENLY. BY LETTING THE DOUGH RISE OVERNIGHT, ALL THAT'S LEFT TO DO THE NEXT MORNING IS TO BAKE THE BUNS. IN THE BLINK OF AN EYE, THERE THEY ARE—CRISP AND WARM ON THE BREAKFAST TABLE.

★ *Make-ahead*   ★ *Wood stove*   ★ *Winter picnic*

½ CUP (100 ML) WARM MILK
½ CUP (100 ML) WATER
1 TSP SUGAR
2 TSP ACTIVE DRY YEAST OR
21 G (0.75 OZ) FRESH YEAST
9 OZ (250 G) ALL-PURPOSE FLOUR OR
LIGHT SPELT FLOUR
½ TSP SALT

OPTIONAL:
2 TBSP WALNUTS

TRY THIS SOMETIME:
TOP SOME, OR ALL, OF THE BUNS
WITH A SPRINKLING OF SESAME SEEDS,
PUMPKIN SEEDS, CORIANDER SEEDS,
OR POPPY SEEDS

The night before, place the warm milk, water, and sugar in a small bowl. Stir to combine. Add the yeast and stir until it is completely dissolved. Let stand briefly until it bubbles. In a bowl combine the flour and salt, then stir in the yeast mixture. Knead for about 10 minutes until the dough is smooth and elastic. If you are using walnuts, break them up coarsely with your hands and knead them into the dough. Cover the bowl, refrigerate, and let the dough rise overnight (10–12 hours).

The next morning, line a baking tray with parchment paper (or, even better, scatter some semolina over the tray). Shape the dough into 4–6 buns. Place the buns on the baking tray; if desired, top with 1–2 teaspoons of seeds. Position the tray on the middle rack of a cold oven. Heat the oven to 425 °F (220 °C) or fire up the wood stove. Bake for 30 minutes or until golden brown.

MAKES 1 LOAF

Paillasse-style bread

THIS IS A VERY TASTY, VERY OLD, AND VERY SIMPLE BREAD RECIPE.
CHARACTERISTIC OF PAILLASSE-STYLE BREAD IS THE LONG, COLD RISE. THIS
BREAD ALWAYS TURNS OUT WELL AND, LIKE ALL BREADS, TASTES BEST
FRESHLY BAKED IN A WOOD-FIRED OVEN OR ON A BAKING STONE.

Wood stove   *Winter picnic*

1 ¼ LB (550 G) ALL-PURPOSE FLOUR
OR PASTRY FLOUR
2 TSP SALT
⅓ OZ (10 G) FRESH YEAST, OR
⅓ TSP ACTIVE DRY YEAST

The night before, in a large bowl place the flour and
salt. Add the yeast (if using fresh, crumble it first).
Working gradually, add about 1 ¼ cup (300 ml) ice-cold
water to the bowl. Knead the dough until it is smooth
and elastic. Cover the bowl and let the dough rise in the
refrigerator overnight.

First thing next morning, preheat the oven to 475 °F
(240 °C). Line a baking tray with parchment paper
or place a baking stone in the oven. Transfer the dough
to a floured work surface. Divide it into 2 equal pieces
and shape into 2 baguettes, each about 12 inches
(30 cm) long. Twist each baguette twice.

Fill a heatproof bowl with hot water and place it in
the oven. Place the loaves on the baking stone or baking
tray. Bake for about 15 minutes, then lower the heat
to 400 °F (200 °C) and bake for another 15 minutes
or until light golden brown.

TIP

You can customize your bread by adding finely chopped sun-dried tomatoes,
chopped olives, rosemary, or coarsely chopped walnuts.

Winter smoothies

THESE SMOOTHIES HELP YOU
FACE WINTER BY PROVIDING YOU
WITH PLENTY OF VITAMINS AND
MINERALS DURING THE DARKEST
TIME OF YEAR. AN ADDED BONUS
IS THAT THESE FRESH BURSTS
OF FLAVOR TURN NOTORIOUS
MORNING GRUMPS INTO GOOD-
HUMORED WINTER ENTHUSIASTS.

★ *Quick* ★ *Immune booster*

SANTA'S HAT
RED BEET WITH A CREAMY TOPPING

1 RED BEET   1 PEAR   ¾ IN (2 CM) PIECE GINGER   2 TBSP WALNUTS OR WALNUT OIL
¾ CUP (200 ML) WATER   1 TBSP WHIPPED CREAM OR SOUR CREAM FOR TOPPING

HOT STAG
APPLE, PEAR, AND LAMB'S LETTUCE

1 APPLE   1 PEAR   1 CUP LAMB'S LETTUCE (MÂCHE)   PINCH OF CHILI POWDER
½ TSP OLIVE OIL   ¾ CUP (200 ML) WATER

OLD SWEDE
BLUEBERRIES, CRANBERRIES, AND YOGURT

1 ½ CUPS (7 OZ/200 G) BLUEBERRIES   1 BANANA   1 TSP DARK HONEY
1 TSP CRANBERRIES   ⅔ CUP (150 G) YOGURT   ¾ CUP (200 ML) OF WATER

COLD KILLER
TANGY ORANGE, CARROT, AND GINGER

2 CARROTS   JUICE OF 4 ORANGES AND 1 LEMON   ¾ IN (2 CM) PIECE GINGER
PINCH OF TURMERIC   ½ TSP OLIVE OIL   2 TSP HONEY   ¾ CUP (200 ML) HOT WATER

Wash and/or peel the raw ingredients, as needed, and cut them into small pieces.
Place all the ingredients in a blender. Blend well, slowly adding the water as you blend.
Divide the smoothie between 2 glasses and enjoy immediately!

THIS HEARTY BREAKFAST WILL MAKE YOU FEEL LIKE YOU ARE IN AN ALPINE HUT,
NO MATTER WHERE YOU'VE PREPARED IT—AT HOME OR ON THE ROAD.
IT IS BEST ENJOYED STRAIGHT OUT OF A CAST-IRON SKILLET OR AN ENAMELED
PAN SO EVERYONE CAN HELP THEMSELVES! SERVE WITH THICK SLICES
OF RUSTIC FARMER'S BREAD SLATHERED WITH BUTTER.

Alpine breakfast hash

SERVES 2

★ Quick   ★ Vegetarian   ★ Energy

2–3 MEDIUM POTATOES, PRECOOKED
OR LEFTOVER FROM THE DAY BEFORE
2 TBSP OLIVE OIL
1 SMALL WHITE OR RED ONION
½ BUNCH CHIVES AND/OR SPRING
ONIONS
½ TBSP BUTTER
2 EGGS
SALT AND BLACK PEPPER
½ BUNCH PARSLEY, CHOPPED

OPTIONAL:
DICED SMOKED BACON, OLIVES,
DICED TOMATOES

Peel and thickly slice the potatoes. In a cast-iron
skillet or heavy enameled pan, heat the olive
oil. Add the potatoes and cook until golden brown.
If you are using bacon, add it now. Peel the onion,
dice or thinly slice it, and add it to the potatoes.
Chop the chives or spring onions and add
to the skillet. Stir in the butter. Beat the eggs
and pour them into the pan. Stir in the tomatoes
and olives, if using. Season with salt (if using bacon,
be careful; it's salty!) and plenty of pepper, and
sprinkle with chopped parsley.

☞ If you like spicy food, pour a generous amount of sriracha sauce over the hash.

Breakfast for late risers

WHEN THE WEATHER IS BAD OR THE AVALANCHE CONDITIONS UNFAVORABLE,
AND YOU FEEL LIKE SLEEPING IN FOR A CHANGE, ALLOW YOURSELF SOME DOWNTIME
AND SPEND A COZY DAY INDOORS. THE BEST START FOR A LAZY DAY IS A RICHLY
SET TABLE AND A DRAWN-OUT, LEISURELY BREAKFAST.

SERVES 2

★ *Quick*   ★ *Winter picnic*

BLUEBERRY PANCAKES

7 OZ (200 G) SPELT FLOUR
2 TBSP CANE SUGAR
PINCH OF SALT
1 ½ TSP BAKING POWDER
1 ½ CUPS MILK
2 EGGS
4 TBSP SUNFLOWER OIL
4 ½ OZ (125 G) OF FRESH BLUEBERRIES
4 TBSP SOUR CREAM
½ TSP VANILLA SUGAR

Combine the flour, sugar, salt, and baking powder in a bowl. Stir in enough milk to make a smooth batter, then stir in the remaining milk, the eggs, and the oil. Grease a non-stick skillet and heat. Working in batches, drop batter to make pancakes about ½-inch (1 ¼ cm) thick. Cook until golden brown on the bottom. Scatter a few blueberries over each pancake, then flip and cook the other side. Sweeten the sour cream with the vanilla sugar and serve it with the pancakes. Alternatively, top the pancakes with honey or maple syrup.

VARIATIONS

PANCAKES WITH CARAMELIZED PEARS:
Peel, core, and slice 2–3 pears. Before cooking the pancakes, add pear slices and 2 teaspoons cane sugar to the skillet and cook until they start to caramelize. Then, ladle the batter over the pears, and cook as above.

BUTTERMILK PANCAKES WITH CRANBERRIES:
Replace half of the milk with buttermilk. Cook pancakes as above, then serve dusted with powdered sugar and topped with cranberry preserves.

★ *Deluxe*   ★ *Energy*

POTATO PANCAKES
WITH SMOKED SALMON

4 LARGE, WAXY POTATOES, SUCH AS YUKON GOLD
½ ONION
SALT AND BLACK PEPPER
4 TBSP VEGETABLE OIL
4 SLICES SMOKED SALMON
2 TBSP SOUR CREAM
½ BUNCH CHIVES

Peel and coarsely grate the potatoes. Place them in a sieve and squeeze out as much liquid as possible. Peel and finely chop the onion. Mix it into the grated potatoes and season with salt and pepper. Heat a small non-stick skillet or cast-iron pan well, then add 2 tablespoons of the oil. Spread half the potato mixture over the bottom of the skillet and lightly press to flatten it. Cook both sides over medium heat until golden brown and crispy. Drain on paper towels and keep warm. Repeat with the second potato pancake. Serve with the smoked salmon on the side. Garnish with sour cream and chives.

POTATO PANCAKES VARIATIONS

SWEET POTATO AND GINGER:
Replace the potatoes with 2 sweet potatoes, and grate a small piece of ginger into the potato mixture. Serve with fresh goat cheese and honey.

SMOKED BACON AND FRIED EGGS:
Add 2 tablespoons of diced bacon to the potato mixture. Cook the pancakes until nice and crispy, then top with a fried egg.

GRUYÈRE AND WALNUTS:
Add ½ cup grated Gruyère cheese and 2 tablespoons chopped walnuts to the potato mixture. Garnish the pancakes with chives.

APPLE AND CINNAMON:
Add 1 peeled and grated apple to the potato mixture. Cook the potato pancakes as above, then serve sprinkled with cinnamon sugar. Garnish with sour cream or yogurt.

THERMOS FILLERS

THERMOS FILLERS

WHETHER YOU PACK SOUP OR STEW IN A THERMOS BECAUSE
YOU ARE GOING ON AN ADVENTURE FAR AWAY FROM CIVILIZATION,
OR BECAUSE YOU SIMPLY WANT TO AVOID BUYING READY-MADE, OVERPRICED,
OFTEN INFERIOR MEALS AT SKI CHALETS, DISHES WELL-SUITED TO A
THERMOS CAN EASILY BE PREPARED AHEAD. AND THEY ARE CALLED COMFORT FOOD
FOR A REASON: THEY WARM BODY AND SOUL ON A COLD WINTER'S DAY AND
MAKE YOU HAPPY. OF COURSE, NO NEED TO BATTLE THE ELEMENTS—YOU
CAN ALSO SIMPLY ENJOY THESE FABULOUS DISHES AT HOME
IN FRONT OF A CRACKLING FIRE!

TIP

Pack the garnishes and additions separately in small containers.
It will keep them from getting soggy, and you will be able to savor the full taste experience outdoors.
Add boiling water to your thermos before filling it. Pour out the water after a couple of minutes,
and fill the thermos with soup or stew. Your food will stay hot even longer!

THIS SPLENDID ASIAN SOUP WARMS INSIDE AND OUT. ON BAD WEATHER DAYS,
IT IS THE ULTIMATE DISH FOR STRENGTHENING YOUR IMMUNE SYSTEM.

Carrot soup
WITH GINGER AND HONEY

SERVES 2

1 MEDIUM ONION

1–2 GARLIC CLOVES

1 IN (2 ½ CM) PIECE OF GINGER

6–8 CARROTS

1 TBSP PEANUT OIL

1 TBSP SESAME OIL

1 TBSP CURRY POWDER (OR ½ TBSP CURRY POWDER AND ½ TBSP TURMERIC)

1–2 TBSP HONEY

2 CUPS (500 ML) VEGETABLE STOCK

2 KAFFIR LIME LEAVES (OPTIONAL)

1 ¾ CUPS (400 ML) COCONUT MILK

SALT AND BLACK PEPPER

FRESH RED CHILI PEPPERS (OPTIONAL)

½ BUNCH OF PARSLEY OR CILANTRO (OPTIONAL)

Peel and finely chop the onion, garlic, and ginger. Peel and slice the carrots.
If you like your soup spicier, thinly slice a few red chilies. In a large saucepan, add the oil
and vegetables and sauté. Stir in the curry powder and the honey. Add the stock and deglaze
by scraping up the brown bits. Cover and simmer over medium heat until the carrots are tender.
Purée the soup using an immersion blender. Add the kaffir lime leaves, if using, then pour
in the coconut milk. Season to taste with salt and pepper and briefly return the soup to a boil.

Serve garnished with chopped parsley or cilantro, if desired.
Chicken satay or grilled shrimp go very well with this soup.

★ *Warming*   ★ *Winter picnic*

Horseradish soup

SERVES 2

1 MEDIUM ONION
1 GARLIC CLOVE
1 STARCHY POTATO OR 1 TBSP FLOUR
2 TBSP SUNFLOWER OIL (OR, EVEN BETTER, 2 TBSP BUTTER)
HANDFUL OF DICED WHITE ROOT VEGETABLES (CELERY ROOT, PARSNIP, OR SIMILAR)
⅛ CUP (60 ML) WHITE WINE
2 CUPS (500 ML) BEEF STOCK (PAGE 188), OR ORGANIC VEGETABLE STOCK
1 CUP (200 G) HEAVY CREAM
SALT AND BLACK PEPPER
½ FRESH HORSERADISH ROOT
1 TBSP CHOPPED PARSLEY AND CHIVES, FOR GARNISH

Peel and finely chop the onion and garlic. Peel and thinly slice the potato. Heat the oil or butter in a pot. Add the vegetables and sauté. (If you are using flour instead of the potato to bind the soup, dust it over the vegetables now.) Deglaze by adding the wine and stock and scraping up the brown bits. Cover the pot and simmer over medium heat until the vegetables are tender. Using an immersion blender, purée the soup. Stir in the cream and season generously with salt and pepper. Peel and finely grate the horseradish. Stir in a handful of horseradish just before serving.

To serve, garnish the soup with the chopped herbs and some additional horseradish. Gruyère croutons (page 105) also taste especially good with the soup.

TIP

Hold the pot on a slight angle as you purée the soup. This will keep the blender submerged and prevent the soup from splattering, while also ensuring that the blender makes contact with all the vegetable chunks ending up in the bottom corner of the pot.

Chicken stew

SERVES 2

2 CHICKEN LEGS (THIGH AND
DRUMSTICK)
SALT AND BLACK PEPPER
6 SHALLOTS
2 GARLIC CLOVES
10 OZ (300 G) MINI POTATOES
1 RED BELL PEPPER
1 ZUCCHINI
½ FENNEL BULB
3 TOMATOES
2 TBSP OLIVE OIL
2 SPRIGS EACH ROSEMARY AND THYME
½ CUP (125 ML) WHITE WINE
2 CUPS (500 ML) ORGANIC VEGETABLE
OR BEEF STOCK (PAGE 188)
1 SMALL RED CHILI PEPPER
½ BUNCH PARSLEY

Preheat the oven to 400 °F (200 °C). Pat the
chicken legs dry with paper towels and season
with salt and pepper. Peel and slice the shallots
into rings. Peel and finely chop the garlic cloves.
Wash and cube the potatoes. Wash, trim, and
slice the bell pepper. Wash and cut the remaining
vegetables into pieces. Heat the oil in a Dutch
oven or other heavy ovenproof pot with a tight-fitting
lid. Add the chicken legs and brown on all sides;
remove and set aside. Add the shallots and garlic
to the pot and sauté until soft and translucent.
Add the vegetables, rosemary, and thyme,
and sweat briefly. Add the white wine and stock,
and deglaze by scraping up the brown bits.
Return the chicken to the pot, then add the chili
pepper. Season everything generously with
more salt and pepper.

Cover the pot with a tight-fitting lid and transfer
to the oven. Braise the stew until the chicken
is cooked through, about 35 minutes. Remove
the chicken, place it on a heatproof plate or pan,
and return it to the oven to crisp up. If you
are transferring the stew to a thermos, pick the
meat from the bones and cut it into small pieces.

Serve garnished with chopped parsley (an extra
dollop of sour cream, a few croutons,
or 2 to 3 teaspoons of pesto also work well).

CHUNKY
Potato stew

THIS STEW IS ONE OF MY THERMOS FILLER FAVORITES.

SERVES 2

5 MEDIUM WAXY POTATOES, SUCH AS YUKON GOLD
2–3 SHALLOTS
1 GARLIC CLOVE
1 LEEK
1 TBSP SUNFLOWER OIL OR BUTTER
½ TBSP DRIED OR 1 TBSP FRESH OREGANO
½ TSP TURMERIC
2 CUPS (500 ML) VEGETABLE OR BEEF STOCK
SALT AND BLACK PEPPER
½ CUP SOUR CREAM
1 BUNCH PARSLEY

Peel the potatoes. Cut 3 of the potatoes into cubes and finely dice the remaining 2. Peel and finely chop the shallots and garlic. Wash the leek well, dice the light green part, and roughly slice the white part. Heat the oil in a large saucepan. Add the onions, shallots, and white part of the leek, and sauté. Add the potato cubes, oregano, and turmeric. Deglaze with the stock and bring to a boil. Season with salt and pepper, and cover. Simmer over medium heat, until the potatoes are tender. Stir in half of the sour cream. Purée the stew with an immersion blender. Return to a boil, add the diced potatoes, and simmer until tender. Add the green part of the leek. Chop the parsley and stir half of it into the stew.

Serve each bowl topped with a dollop of sour cream and garnished with the remaining chopped parsley. If you are packing the stew into a thermos, stir everything together first.

Sliced dark farmer's bread, such as the one on page 60, is ideal with this dish. You can also add your favorite soup garnishes from pages 105–107. I think Gruyère croutons taste especially good: I fry them together with finely diced smoked bacon, and this adds a bit of crunch to the stew. Other flavorful additions are a few thin strips of smoked salmon or slices of fried salsiccia sausage.

Cream of squash soup

THIS SOUP IS A TRUE FALL AND WINTER CLASSIC. IT IS HEALTHY AND QUICK
TO MAKE, AND IT NEVER FAILS TO PLEASE. GIVEN THE EASE OF PREPARATION AND ITS
LOVELY COLOR, I LIKE TO USE HOKKAIDO SQUASH. EVERY BIT OF THIS TYPE OF SQUASH
CAN BE USED, EVEN THE PEEL. MUSCAT SQUASH OR BUTTERNUT SQUASH ALSO
TASTE REALLY GOOD BUT WILL NEED TO BE PEELED.

SERVES 4

1 HOKKAIDO SQUASH
(1 ⅓ LB – 1 ¾ LB / 600 – 800 G)
½ ONION
1 – 2 GARLIC CLOVES
1 IN (2 ½ CM) PIECE OF GINGER
2 TBSP OLIVE OR CANOLA OIL
⅛ CUP (60 ML) WHITE WINE
2 CUPS (500 ML) VEGETABLE STOCK
1 CUP (200 G) HEAVY CREAM
½ TSP CORIANDER SEEDS,
WHOLE OR GROUND
SALT AND BLACK PEPPER
PUMPKIN SEEDS AND PUMPKIN
SEED OIL, FOR GARNISH

OPTIONAL:
½ BUNCH PARSLEY,
FRESH RED CHILI PEPPERS

Wash the squash and cut it in half. Using a spoon, scoop out the seeds. If you are not using a Hokkaido squash, peel the squash. Cube the flesh. Peel and finely chop the onion and garlic. Peel and chop the ginger. If you like more heat, thinly slice a few chili peppers. Heat the oil in a large pot. Add the onion, garlic, and ginger, and sauté. Add the squash and sweat it briefly. Add the wine and deglaze by scraping up the brown bits. Pour in the stock and bring to a boil. Cover and simmer over medium heat until the squash is tender. Purée the soup well with an immersion blender.

Stir in the cream. Season generously to taste with coriander seeds, salt, and pepper. Return to the boil and add a bit more stock, if needed, to obtain the desired consistency.

Dry-toast the pumpkin seeds with a pinch of salt. To serve, scatter the pumpkin seeds and some chopped parsley, if using, over the soup. Drizzle with a few drops of pumpkin seed oil. The soup looks especially attractive with a dollop of whipped cream on top, which then slowly melts.

TIP

Always thin puréed soups with a bit of stock at the end of the cooking time. If you add too much liquid at the beginning, the soup will not be as creamy.

Add salt to the soup only at the end of the cooking time. If you have seasoned with too much salt early on, you will have to thin the soup too much, and then it will not be as creamy.

A CULT ALPINE CLASSIC IS GIVEN NEW LIFE! THIS PERFECT
PEA SOUP TASTES MARVELOUSLY FRESH.
IT ALSO HELPS TO FREE UP THE RESPIRATORY TRACT.

FRESH
Pea soup
WITH EGG AND SAUSAGE

SERVES 4

2 EGGS   2 SMALL COOKED SAUSAGES, SUCH AS GERMAN OR
AUSTRIAN WURST   1 MEDIUM ONION
1 TBSP BUTTER   1 LB 2 OZ (500 G) FROZEN PEAS
300 ML VEGETABLE STOCK   ½ ORGANIC LEMON
½ BUNCH MINT   1 BUNCH PARSLEY
PINCH OF CAYENNE PEPPER   SALT AND BLACK PEPPER
½ CUP PLAIN GREEK YOGURT   COARSELY GROUND BLACK PEPPER

Place the eggs in boiling water and cook for about
8 minutes, or until hard-boiled. Cool the eggs in cold
water, then peel and chop them. Place the sausages
in the egg water to heat, but don't let the water
boil or the wurst will burst! In the meantime, peel and
chop the onion. Heat the butter in a large saucepan,
add the onion, and sauté until soft and translucent.
Add the peas and sauté briefly. Pour in the stock and
bring to a boil. Lower heat and simmer for 6–8 minutes.

Wash, zest, and juice the lemon. Wash and chop the
herbs (reserving a few mint leaves for garnish), then
add them to the soup. Purée the soup immediately with
an immersion blender. Season to taste with cayenne
pepper, salt, and black pepper. Add the lemon juice
to the yogurt and mix until smooth. Slice the sausages

and divide them among bowls or soup plates. Ladle
hot soup into the bowls. Using a spoon, swirl some
yogurt mixture into each bowl. Garnish with chopped
egg, a bit of lemon zest, mint leaves, and a sprinkling
of coarsely ground black pepper.

VEGETARIAN VERSION
Replace the sausage with cubes of fried halloumi
cheese and toasted walnuts.

HEARTIER VERSION
Add diced potatoes to the soup and cook until tender.
Add some whole peas to the soup. Fry 1 tablespoon diced
bacon until crisp and scatter over each bowl.

Sweet potato soup

WITH FRESH CHILIES

THIS FIERY DELIGHT HAS A SLIGHTLY ASIAN TOUCH, SPREADS A NICE WARMTH INSIDE,
AND IS GUARANTEED TO MAKE TIRED LEGS COME TO LIFE AGAIN.

INGREDIENTS

SERVES 2

3 MEDIUM SWEET POTATOES
1 MEDIUM ONION
1 – 2 GARLIC CLOVES
1 – 2 FRESH MILD RED CHILI PEPPERS,
SUCH AS PEPPERONCINI, AJI DULCE,
OR JALAPEÑO
1 TBSP EACH PEANUT OIL AND SESAME
OIL (OR SUNFLOWER OIL)
2 CUPS (500 ML) VEGETABLE STOCK
1 ORGANIC LIME
1 ¾ CUPS (400 ML) COCONUT MILK
SALT AND BLACK PEPPER
2 TBSP SOUR CREAM
½ BUNCH CILANTRO, CHOPPED

PREPERATION

Peel the sweet potatoes and cut them into small pieces.
Peel and dice the onion and garlic. Wash and very
thinly slice the chili peppers. (For a milder soup, seed
the peppers first.) Heat the oil in a large saucepan.
Add the onion, garlic, and chili pepper and sauté. Add
three-quarters of the sweet potatoes. Add the stock and
deglaze by scraping up the browned bits. Cover and
simmer over medium heat until the potatoes are tender.
Purée the soup with an immersion blender, then add the
remaining sweet potatoes. Simmer until potatoes are
cooked through but still slightly firm to the bite.

Wash, zest, and juice the lime. Add the coconut milk
to the soup, and season to taste with salt and pepper.
Return briefly to a boil, then stir in the lime juice.

Add the lime zest to the sour cream and mix. To serve,
top soup with a dollop of sour cream and a sprinkle
of chopped cilantro. Pita Bread with Sesame and Nigella
(page 67) is a perfect match for this soup.

Bread soup
WITH BEER

THIS MARVELOUS, SIMPLE-YET-DELICIOUS SOUP IS A TRADITIONAL DISH THAT
EVEN MY GRANDMOTHER MADE. IT'S A GOOD WAY TO USE UP STALE BREAD,
PLUS IT GIVES YOU PLENTY OF ENERGY FOR THE NEXT SNOWBALL FIGHT.

SERVES 4

1 MEDIUM WHITE ONION
1 GARLIC CLOVE
7 OZ (200 G) DAY-OLD BREAD
(DARK SPICED FARMER'S BREAD
WORKS BEST)
2 RIPE TOMATOES
2 TBSP SUNFLOWER OIL
(OR, FOR A MORE LUXURIOUS SOUP,
2 TBSP BUTTER)
1 CUP (250 ML) BEER
(LIGHT, DARK, OR WHEAT BEER); FINISH
OFF THE BOTTLE WHILE YOU COOK
3 CUPS (750 ML) BEEF STOCK
(PAGE 188) OR ORGANIC
VEGETABLE STOCK
½ CUP (100 G) HEAVY CREAM
FINELY CHOPPED MIXED HERBS, SUCH
AS CHIVES, PARSLEY, AND MARJORAM
SALT AND BLACK PEPPER
PINCH OF NUTMEG (OPTIONAL)

Peel and finely chop the onion and garlic. Cube the
bread and tomatoes. Heat the oil or butter in a
pot. Add the onion and garlic, and sauté until soft and
translucent. Add the bread and tomatoes and cook
for a few minutes. Pour in the beer and stock. Simmer
for about 10 minutes. Using a potato masher or a
cooking spoon, mash everything in the pot until smooth
and creamy. Add the cream and herbs. Season
to taste with salt and pepper. If you like, grate a pinch
of nutmeg into the soup.

Sprinkle with additional chopped herbs and serve.

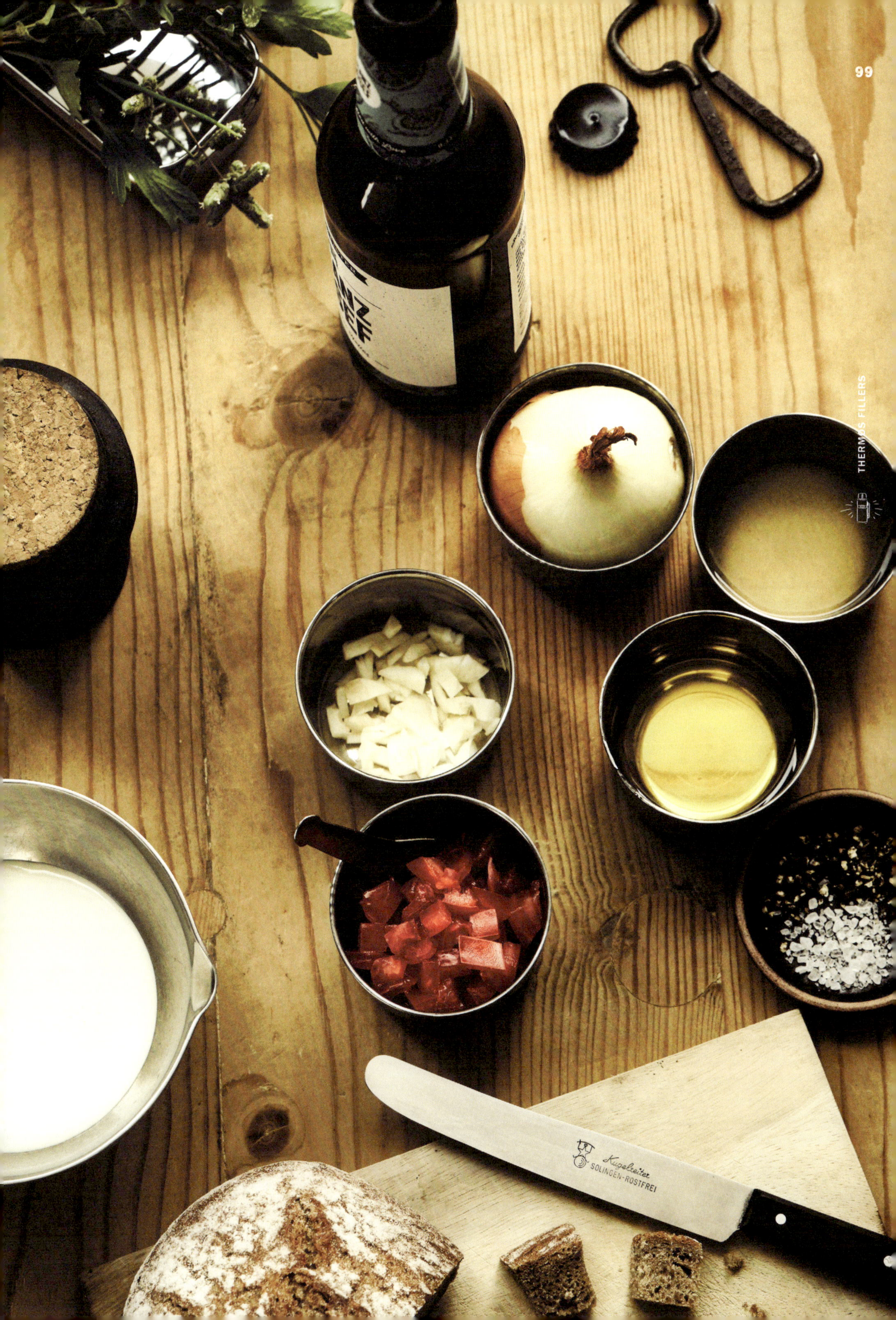
Kugelreiter
SOLINGEN-ROSTFREI

A GOOD CLEAR SOUP ALWAYS HAS A FLAVORFUL STOCK AS ITS BASE.
THERE IS A RECIPE FOR A RICH BEEF STOCK ON PAGE 188.
THE DELICIOUS HERBED CREPES USED IN THIS SOUP (PAGE 106) ARE QUICK TO MAKE.
CREPE SOUP TURNS FESTIVE AND EVEN TASTIER WITH SEVERAL DIFFERENT GARNISHES,
SUCH AS RED BEET SEMOLINA DUMPLINGS (PAGE 105), ADDED TO THE BROTH.

★ *Quick*   ★ *Make-ahead*

Crepe soup

SERVES 2

INGREDIENTS

2 CUPS (500 ML) BEEF STOCK (PAGE 188)
OR ORGANIC VEGETABLE STOCK
1–2 CUPS THINLY SLICED HERBED CREPES (PAGE 106)
SALT AND BLACK PEPPER
1 TBSP SWEET SHERRY OR MARSALA, OR TO TASTE
1 HANDFUL EACH FINELY CHOPPED CHIVES AND PARSLEY

PREPERATION

Heat the stock in a pot. Roll up the crepes to thinly
slice them. Add the crepe slices to the stock for a few minutes
until heated through. Season the soup with salt and pepper.
Add the sherry or Marsala. Divide the soup among 2 bowls.
Sprinkle with chives and parsley, and serve.

VARIATION ★ *Deluxe*

Purchase 9 oz (250 g) of veal sausage meat from the butcher. Thinly spread the meat over the
crepes and roll them up. Wrap crepes tightly in plastic wrap, then in aluminum foil. Twist
both ends closed, like wrapped candies. Fill a large pot with water and bring to a simmer. Add the
crepe rolls to the pot and simmer for about 15 minutes. Remove from the pot and set aside
to cool. Refrigerate the rolls until ready to use. Unwrap as needed, slice the filled crepes into
very thin rounds, and garnish the soup. This is a fabulous variation for special occasions!

Barley stew

BARLEY, A SPLENDID GRAIN, HAS UNJUSTLY BEEN RELEGATED TO THE SIDELINES.
IT CAN BE COOKED JUST LIKE A RISOTTO RICE, SUCH AS ARBORIO, IT IS EASILY DIGESTED,
RICH IN CARBOHYDRATES, AND IT SATISFIES FOR A LONG TIME.

INGREDIENTS

SERVES 2

2 WAXY POTATOES,
SUCH AS YUKON GOLD
2 CARROTS
½ LEEK
½ ONION
2 ¾ OZ (75 G) FROZEN PEAS
OR 2 KALE LEAVES
3 ½ OZ (100 G) PEARL BARLEY
2 TBSP OLIVE OR CANOLA OIL
2 – 3 CUPS (500 – 600 ML) BEEF STOCK
OR ORGANIC VEGETABLE STOCK
1 BAY LEAF
1 THICK SLICE OF COOKED HAM
SALT AND PEPPER
½ BUNCH PARSLEY

PREPERATION

Peel the potatoes and carrots and cut them into ½-inch (1 ¼ cm) cubes. Wash, trim, and slice the leek. Peel and finely dice the onion. If using kale, wash, trim, and coarsely chop it. Place the barley in a sieve and rinse thoroughly. Heat the oil in a large pot. Add the onion and sauté until soft and translucent. Add the barley, stock, and bay leaf, and bring to a boil. Simmer over low heat for 15 minutes. Add the potatoes, then add the remaining vegetables gradually according to their cooking times. Cook until the barley and potatoes are tender. Slice the ham into diamond-shaped pieces, then add to the stew until heated through. Season to taste with salt and pepper. Serve garnished with chopped parsley.

VEGETARIAN VERSION

Cubes of smoked tofu are an excellent substitute for the ham. Give it a try!

HEARTIER VERSION

Fry up some spicy sausage, such as chorizo or merguez, cut it into pieces, and add alongside the ham.

Soup garnishes

THE NEXT FEW RECIPES MAKE TASTY GARNISHES TO BRIGHTEN UP AND
REFINE YOUR SOUPS AND STEWS. WHETHER YOUR MEAL IS TO BE SAVORED AT HOME,
IN A COZY MOUNTAIN CABIN, OR OUT OF A THERMOS IN THE GREAT OUTDOORS,
CHOOSE THE GARNISH THAT APPEALS TO YOU THE MOST.

GRUYÈRE CROUTONS

2 SLICES DAY-OLD FARMER'S BREAD (OR ANY OTHER HEARTY DARK BREAD)
4 TBSP CLARIFIED BUTTER OR VEGETABLE OIL
2 TBSP GRATED GRUYÈRE CHEESE
SALT AND BLACK PEPPER

Remove the crusts from the bread and cut it into cubes.
In a cast-iron or non-stick skillet, heat the butter or oil.
Add the bread and shake the pan back and forth. Season with salt and a bit of pepper.
When the croutons begin to brown, add the cheese.
When the cheese melts, transfer the croutons to paper towels to drain and let cool.
Serve immediately or store the croutons in an airtight container.

Gruyère croutons are perfect with Horseradish Soup (page 83)
or Chunky Potato Stew (page 87).

RED BEET
SEMOLINA DUMPLINGS
WITH TOASTED WALNUTS

3 TBSP JARRED RED BEETS   1 TBSP HEAVY CREAM   2 TBSP WALNUTS
2 TBSP (30 G) SOFTENED BUTTER   1 EGG AT ROOM TEMPERATURE
SALT   FRESHLY GRATED NUTMEG   ⅓ CUP (90 G) DURUM WHEAT SEMOLINA

Combine the beets and cream in a beaker or other deep cup, and purée using an immersion blender. In a dry skillet, toast the walnuts then finely chop or grind them. Place the butter, egg, salt, and a pinch of nutmeg in a bowl, and whisk until foamy. Stir in the beet and cream mixture, then the walnuts. Gradually stir in the semolina. Let the mixture stand briefly.

Place 4 cups (1 l) of lightly salted water in a pot and bring to a boil. Fill a cup with cold water. Using 2 teaspoons that you moisten in the water, form small dumplings from the semolina mixture. Slide the dumplings into the boiling water and reduce the heat. When all the dumplings have floated to the surface, remove the pot from the heat and let the dumplings cook for 5 – 10 minutes more. Serve immediately or transfer the dumplings into a container of cold, lightly salted water, and refrigerate.

These dumplings taste really good in Horseradish Soup (page 83) or in a flavorful stock (page 188), to which you can add additional garnish combinations.
They also make an attractive (and quick) appetizer when tossed in a bit of brown butter and topped with arugula and grated Parmesan.

HERBED CREPES

3 ½ OZ (100 G) SPELT FLOUR, ½ CUP (100 ML) MILK, 2 EGGS, SALT, BLACK PEPPER,
4 TBSP CHOPPED FRESH HERBS (SUCH AS CHIVES, DILL, PARSLEY, BASIL),
CANOLA OR OLIVE OIL (FOR COOKING)

Place the flour in a bowl. Add a bit of milk and stir until smooth. Stir in the remaining milk, eggs, salt, and pepper, and sprinkle in the herbs. Heat a non-stick skillet and lightly grease it. Working in batches, ladle batter into the skillet and cook until brown on both sides.

Stack the crepes on a plate and let cool. To make the garnish for Crepe Soup (page 100), roll up the crepes and slice very thinly.

TOASTED PUMPKIN SEEDS

Pumpkin seeds (pepitas) are delicious as a stand-alone trail snack or in
many soups. They are the traditional garnish for Cream of Squash Soup (page 88).
Heat a dry skillet on the stovetop. Add the seeds and a bit of salt.
Shake back and forth until the seeds begin to crackle and brown.
Transfer to a plate and let cool.

GLAZED CHESTNUTS

1 TBSP SUGAR
5 ½ OZ (150 G) SHELLED COOKED CHESTNUTS
(ALSO AVAILABLE VACUUM-PACKED)
1 TBSP BUTTER

Heat a deep skillet. Add the sugar and 1 teaspoon of water and stir.
Boil until the sugar has dissolved. Coarsely chop the chestnuts and add them to the skillet.
Stirring constantly, or shaking the pan back and forth, cook the chestnuts until
golden brown and caramelized. Transfer to a plate to cool completely.
Try them with Bread Soup with Beer (page 98), Sweet Potato Soup with Fresh Chilies
(page 92), or Cream of Squash Soup (page 88).

These chestnuts also shine as a garnish for a festive roast duck or goose!

WINTER TRAIL SNACKS

WINTER TRAIL SNACKS

WHEN YOU ARE WALKING UP A MOUNTAIN ON BACKCOUNTRY SKIS
OR PULLING A SLED BEHIND YOU, TRAIL SNACKS THAT ARE BOTH DELICIOUS
AND ENERGY-BOOSTING ARE QUITE WELCOME. THEY NOT ONLY HELP YOU
MAINTAIN STRENGTH BUT ALSO SAVE TIME WHEN YOU ARE SWEATING HEAVILY AND
DON'T HAVE TIME FOR A LONG FOOD BREAK. OFF THE MOUNTAIN, THESE SNACKS
CAN DOUBLE AS ATTRACTIVE LITTLE GIFTS WHEN NICELY PACKAGED.

Winter trail mixes

TRAIL MIXES ARE AN ESSENTIAL PART OF ANY OUTDOOR
ACTIVITY. BUT EVEN IN THE URBAN WILDERNESS,
A BAG OF CRUNCHY, HEALTHY, ENERGY-BOOSTING TRAIL MIX
IS ALWAYS WITH ME. AS THEY SAY ON DAYS OF FABULOUS
DEEP POWDER, WHEN BACK ON THE SKI LIFT YET AGAIN,
"NO FRIENDS ON POWDER DAYS"! IN OTHER WORDS,
THERE'S NO STOPPING FOR ANYTHING OR ANYONE—EXCEPT
FOR A QUICK HANDFUL OF AWESOME HOMEMADE TRAIL
MIX TO FUEL THE NEXT DOWNHILL RUN.

AUTUMN STORM

1 ½ OZ (40 G) RAW PECANS
1 ½ OZ (40 G) RAW WALNUTS
1 ½ OZ (40 G) PUMPKIN SEEDS,
DRY-TOASTED WITH A PINCH OF CINNAMON SUGAR
1 ½ OZ (40 G) SHELLED RAW PISTACHIOS
1 ½ OZ (40 G) DRIED APPLE RINGS, CUT INTO PIECES
1 ½ OZ (40 G) DRIED FIGS, CUT INTO PIECES

DEEP POWDER DREAM

3 OZ (80 G) CANDIED ALMONDS (PAGE 121)
1 ½ OZ (40 G) RAW HAZELNUTS
1 ½ OZ (40 G) CHOCOLATE-COVERED RAISINS
1 ½ OZ (40 G) DRIED CHERRIES, HALVED
1 ½ OZ (40 G) UNSWEETENED COCONUT FLAKES

VERY BERRY

1 ½ OZ (40 G) DRIED BLUEBERRIES OR GOJI BERRIES
1 ½ OZ (40 G) RAW ALMONDS
1 ½ OZ (40 G) WHITE CHOCOLATE CHIPS OR CHOPPED WHITE CHOCOLATE
1 ½ OZ (40 G) CASHEWS (SPLIT IN HALF, AS NEEDED)
1 ½ OZ (40 G) DRIED PINEAPPLE OR PINEAPPLE CHIPS, CUT INTO PIECES
1 ½ OZ (40 G) CANDIED GINGER, FINELY DICED

WINTER TRAIL SNACKS

MINI CHOCOLATE BROWNIE BALLS

⋆ Deluxe ⋆ Energy ⋆ Winter picnic

1 CUP (100 G) MIXED RAW PECANS
AND WALNUTS
2 CUPS (200 G) PITTED DATES
2 TBSP DARK COCOA POWDER
SEEDS OF ½ VANILLA BEAN
PINCH OF SALT

OPTIONAL:
2 TBSP COFFEE BEANS, COARSELY
CRUSHED IN A MORTAR AND PESTLE

In a dry skillet, lightly toast the pecans and walnuts. Remove from the pan and set aside to cool. Transfer nuts to a food processor, add remaining ingredients except coffee beans, and process. Moisten your hands with water and shape mixture into walnut-sized balls. If desired, roll the balls in the crushed coffee beans. Let brownie balls cool for about 30 minutes, or freeze briefly to harden.

CARROT CAKE BALLS

⋆ Energy ⋆ Immune booster ⋆ Winter picnic

2 CARROTS
3 OZ (80 G) MIXED RAW ALMONDS
AND WALNUTS
1 CUP (100 G) PITTED DATES
2 TSP DARK HONEY
½ TSP GROUND CINNAMON
½ TSP FRESHLY GRATED GINGER
PINCH OF FRESHLY GRATED NUTMEG
4 TBSP DESICCATED COCONUT

Peel and finely grate the carrots. In a dry skillet, lightly toast the nuts. Let cool. Place all ingredients except the coconut in a food processor and finely chop. Moisten your hands with water and shape mixture into walnut-sized balls. Roll the balls in the coconut. Let cool for about 30 minutes, or freeze briefly to harden.

Energy balls

THESE WINTER ENERGY BALLS ARE ALWAYS A BIG HIT WITH
FRIENDS AND FAMILY ALIKE. IT'S NOT JUST APPEARANCES—THEY TASTE
SUPER FANTASTIC, TOO! AND THEY ALWAYS GIVE YOU A SMALL
BURST OF ENERGY EXACTLY WHEN YOU NEED IT.

MAKES 12–15 SMALL BALLS

DID YOU KNOW ...?
INTERESTING WINTER FACTS

✗ The lowest recorded temperature in Germany to date
was -36 °F (-37.8 °C). It was measured in Hüll, Upper Bavaria
on February 12, 1929.

✗ The lowest recorded temperature in the United States
to date was -80 °F (-62.2 °C). It was measured in Prospect
Creek Camp, Alaska, on January 23, 1971.

✗ The lowest recorded temperature worldwide to date
is a mind-boggling -128.5 °F (-89.2 °C). It was measured
in Wostok, Antarctica, on July 21, 1983.

✗ When you need to melt enough snow to get 4 cups (1 l)
of water for tea, if the snow is fresh you will need a 40-cup
(10 l) saucepan packed full of snow. Melting snow becomes
really arduous when you need 12 cups (3 l) of water
for cooking pasta. Rather than using snow, look around
for transparent, clean ice, which is much denser. The
proportion of water gained from melting ice is almost 1 to 1.

✗ In the northern hemisphere, meteorological winter lasts from the beginning of December to the end of February. In Alpine and very northern regions, the first snowfall can come as early as August, and the last often in late May. Astronomical winter starts on December 21, the winter solstice, and this is when days are at their shortest. The further north, the fewer the hours of daylight. In northern Scandinavia the sun no longer rises, and the darkness of the polar night rules. Astronomical winter ends on March 23, when day and night are equal (the spring equinox). From then on, days get longer than nights again.

✗ When spending time outdoors in winter you lose a great deal of fluids without realizing it. Of course, we all notice our steamy breath in winter, which demonstrates how humidity surrenders to the very dry, cold air. If you are at higher altitudes and moving, you lose up to 2 cups (0.5 l) of fluids per hour just by virtue of breathing. To prevent dehydration and keep your body fit, you must always drink enough fluids—ideally isotonic drinks—in the mountains and the outdoors.

✗ Snow only crunches audibly when you walk on it at about 19 °F (- 7 °C), when snow crystals are brittle and break under your feet. This is always a telltale sign that it's bloody cold outside; who needs a thermometer! In all seriousness, though, the true practical application of this knowledge is that longer periods of very low temperatures can have a negative effect on the snow cover; during extreme cold, the avalanche risk level can rise.

THESE BARS ARE TASTY, HEALTHY, AND VERY PORTABLE.
THEY ARE EASY TO BITE INTO EVEN WHEN IT'S VERY COLD OUTSIDE.
AND THEY'RE SO QUICK THAT YOU CAN EASILY MAKE
ENOUGH BARS AT HOME FOR AN ENTIRE WINTER HOLIDAY. MAKING
THEM WITH KIDS IN THE KITCHEN IS ALSO GREAT FUN.

Fruit bars

SERVES 10–12

★ *Energy* ★ *Immune booster* ★ *Winter picnic*

½ CUP (50 G) PEELED AND
PITTED SOFT DATES
1 CUP (100 G) SOFT DRIED APRICOTS
1 CUP (100 G) SOFT RAISINS
½ CUP (50 G) DRIED CRANBERRIES
4 TBSP APPLE JUICE
1 CUP (100 G) SLIVERED ALMONDS
4 LARGE RECTANGULAR
OBLATEN WAFERS

Using a food processor or an immersion blender, purée the dried fruit and the apple juice until the mixture is smooth and sticky. Place the mixture in a bowl, add the almonds, and mix to combine.

Place 2 wafers on a work surface. Spread half of the mixture about ¾-inch (2 cm) thick on top of each wafer and smooth. Top with remaining 2 wafers. Using a cutting board, gently and evenly press down on the bars so they stick together. Cut the wafers into bars with a sharp knife.

☞ STORAGE

Stored in an airtight container, the bars will keep for 2–3 weeks. Wrap 1–2 pieces at a time in wax paper if you want to take them along.

STORAGE

Allow the almonds to cool completely on a plate or baking tray before storing. Store in a cardboard box or paper bag in a dry place.

Candied almonds

DURING THE FAMOUS *OKTOBERFEST*, IN MUNICH, EATING CANDIED ALMONDS IS A MUST. WHAT'S NOT TO LOVE ABOUT THIS SWEET, CRUNCHY SNACK? BETTER YET, YOU DON'T HAVE TO WAIT UNTIL OCTOBER, SINCE YOU CAN MAKE THEM YOURSELF IN NO TIME AT ALL.

★ *Quick* ★ *Energy*

1 CUP (200 G) SUGAR
2 TBSP VANILLA SUGAR
PINCH OF CINNAMON
7 OZ (200 G) RAW,
SKIN-ON WHOLE ALMONDS

Place about ½ cup water in a saucepan. Add the sugars and a pinch of cinnamon. Bring to a boil, then add the almonds. Stirring constantly, cook until all the water has evaporated. Make sure that all the almonds are evenly caramelized and golden brown. Don't let them get too dark or they will taste bitter. Transfer the almonds to a sheet of parchment paper and let cool. Be careful, they will be very hot!

Salted almonds with red chili

SOME OF YOU ARE SURE TO HAVE SAMPLED A SIMILAR VERSION OF THESE SPICY ALMONDS IN SPANISH TAPAS BARS. THEY MAKE A WONDERFUL SNACK THAT I NEVER GO WITHOUT, WHETHER I'M OUT IN THE MOUNTAINS OR AT HOME SIPPING A GLASS OF RED WINE BY THE CRACKLING FIRE.

★ *Quick* ★ *Energy*

7 OZ (200 G) RAW, SKIN-ON WHOLE
ALMONDS
1 TBSP OLIVE OIL
1–2 DRIED RED CHILIES OR
1 TSP FINELY CHOPPED FRESH
RED CHILI PEPPER
SALT (IDEALLY FLEUR DE SEL)

In a dry skillet, toast the almonds until fragrant. Add the oil and the chilies, cook briefly with the almonds, and season with salt.

IN WINTER, THE DISTINCTIVE AROMA OF ROASTING CHESTNUTS
IS TYPICAL OF MANY A GERMAN MARKET. LOW IN FAT BUT RELATIVELY
HIGH IN CARBOHYDRATES AND PROTEINS, THIS HOT DELICACY IS
A PERFECT SPORT SNACK.

★ Quick ★ Energy

Roasted chestnuts

1 LB 2 OZ (500 G) WHOLE SHELLED CHESTNUTS

Wash the chestnuts. Using a paring knife or other small, sharp knife, cut a cross into the rounded
side of each chestnut. Now off to the hot grill! Roasted chestnuts are best grilled over indirect heat for
about 20 minutes. Use a grilling basket to keep them from rolling away. Chestnuts can also be roasted in the oven.
Preheat to 400 °F (200 °C) and place them on a baking tray. Bake for about 20 minutes.

Every few minutes, spray the chestnuts with a bit of water. Turn constantly to avoid
burning. Spraying with water ensures the shells will burst open and the skin will be easier
to remove afterwards. Peel the chestnuts while they are still hot. Use a kitchen towel to handle
the chestnuts and work quickly, otherwise you will burn your fingers.

★ *Quick* ★ *Deluxe* ★ *Energy*

To make a good thing even better, go with the sweet version and caramelize the roasted chestnuts.

WINTER TRAIL SNACKS

Caramelized chestnuts

1 LB 2 OZ (500 G) WHOLE SHELLED CHESTNUTS
2 ¾ OZ (75 G) BUTTER   1 ¾ OZ (50 G) BROWN SUGAR
PINCH OF CINNAMON   2 TBSP HONEY OR MAPLE SYRUP

Place all the ingredients in a deep skillet.
Stirring constantly, cook until the chestnuts are coated with a shiny brown layer.

STORAGE

Allow the chestnuts to cool completely on a plate or baking tray before storing.
Store in a cardboard box or paper bag in a dry place. But of course, they taste best warm.

Freeriding

AN INTERVIEW WITH JACOBA KRIECHMAYR, AKA JAY

Freeriding is skiing off-piste in the backcountry, in areas usually accessed with a lift. It is absolute, pure skiing, that gives you a feeling of flow. Jacoba, known as Jay, has completely dedicated herself to the flow experience. She's a professional freerider and backcountry skier. In wintertime she ski tours all over the Alps, competes in events, and occasionally goes back to Canada for yet another photo shoot. She comes from a completely ski-crazed family: her father is a state-certified ski instructor who taught skiing; her mother was also a ski instructor; and her brother Vincent is one of Austria's best downhill skiers. Naturally, Jay has been skiing since earliest childhood. Skiing means the world to her.

Today she shows me Obertauern, her home turf. On the lift we get a chance to talk about her life outside the Freeride World Tour Qualifier events and off the slopes. Jay genuinely surprises me with her versatility. A hardened ski professional, she's on her skis almost daily during the ski season. In the short time left the rest of the year, she studies materials science at the university. As a hobby—and a counterbalance—she practices organic gardening on her parents' farm. As soon as our skis are back on, I struggle to keep up with her.

Of course, I'm also eager to learn more about Jay's personal "Great Outdoors" and her cooking skills...

JACOBA — AN INTERVIEW

You are an athlete competing in the Freeride World Tour Qualifier events. How long have you been competing? How many days a year do you spend on your skis, and what other sports do you do to offset skiing and keep yourself in top shape?

I skied my first competition in January 2013 and came in third. Since then, freeride competitions are a part of my life. I don't count the days I spend skiing, but I can tell you that there are very many of them. I usually start the winter off in November and go through May (or beyond, depending on snow conditions) on skis. Even though I don't ski every day, my skis certainly spend more days on my feet than they do stored in the basement...In summer I like to cycle, run, wakeboard, hike in the mountains, or spend time in the power room (also known as the fitness room). I prefer to do sports in the open air. I'm outdoors every day. On the rare day that I don't do any sports, farm work keeps me fit.

What do you always take with you, aside from gear, when you set off on a longer ski trip? Above all, of course, I'm interested in the kind of food you pack.

I always carry a handmade Damascus steel pocket knife with me. It comes in handy on many occasions, but especially on a summit after a climb for cutting bacon into paper-thin slices! (laughs). I always bring a thermos of hot tea. My favorite is fresh ginger and lemon tea for the warmth and energy it provides. To eat, I always have a mixture of nuts and dried fruit with me, and sometimes homemade banana bread. I cannot be without a bar of white chocolate.

What was your best moment in the mountains? What does being in the great outdoors mean to you?

I enjoy every single day I spend in the mountains, and there have been a great many wonderful moments. But most wonderful are the times when the snow is just right, I'm far from the hustle and bustle, far from the cameras and the pressures of competing, just simply shredding. Plenty of good runs, endless powder, a high stoke factor: all of this is best shared with many good friends at home in Obertauern.

Were you ever in a really tricky situation on a mountain? Did this affect you later on?

Yes, I have definitely been in tricky situations, not only because of injury but also avalanches. I badly injured myself in Slovakia during a freeride competition. My evacuation took forever, and the medical care there wasn't the best. Still, it all ended well; the following winter I was back in place at the starting line, ready to compete again.

Also, a few years ago, I triggered a slab avalanche on a slope that I had skied on at least a thousand times before. I made a stupid mistake. I ignored what I knew about the slope's location, the weather, snowpack, and power of the sun's rays at that time of day, just because I wanted a few more turns in the powder. The avalanche swept me up but spit me out again. Thankfully, other than a few bruises, I was unharmed. In an emergency, my friends—who were well-trained and well-equipped—were behind me and could have rescued me. But it was a resounding wake-up call. Since then, I think twice before I ski onto a slope.

Many skiers, mostly young, watch the videos and competitions of professional skiers in backcountry terrain and want to imitate them. What advice do you have for them so they can safely approach this kind of terrain?

Equipment is extremely important. You must always have an avalanche beacon/transceiver, a shovel, probes, and an avalanche airbag pack with you. But just having the right equipment isn't enough—it's also vital to know how to use it properly. This is why I recommend that anyone who enjoys freeriding take a course on how to use avalanche transceivers, how to plan routes, how to evaluate snow conditions, and what to do in an emergency. This knowledge should be refreshed every year before winter starts. Also, undergo beacon/transceiver training at the start of each winter so you know exactly what to do in an emergency.

And let's finally get to the kitchen: what is your best winter dish to get fit for a competition? What is your favorite dish for reloading your batteries once you are back at home?

This is a tough question, because I love eating! I think it's important to use high-quality ingredients, mostly seasonal, and locally produced. I have a very sensitive digestive system. Eating things that don't agree with me weakens me so much that I can't perform at my peak during a competition. This isn't always easy when traveling, but I always enjoy a good piece of organic meat with oven-roasted vegetables. I prefer to make this myself, followed by homemade rice pudding with almond milk, cinnamon, and fruit for dessert. At home in Obertauern, after a successful day, I usually indulge in an onion-and-garlic soup with cheese dumplings at my favorite ski hut. But even on the rare occasion that I don't eat at the ski hut, I will often prepare soups or warm stews for myself. They refuel body and soul perfectly after a long day of skiing.

CARAMELS CONJURE UP WARM CHILDHOOD
MEMORIES, AND THEY CAN BE CUSTOMIZED
BY ADDING BOLD SPICES OR DIFFERENT
GARNISHES UNTIL YOU FIND YOUR FAVORITE.
YOU CAN ALSO WRAP EACH CARAMEL
SEPARATELY (PATIENCE IS A VIRTUE!) FOR
A GREAT GIFT TO OTHERS—OR TO YOURSELF,
WHEN YOU ARE IN THE SNOWY MOUNTAINS.

Quick ★ *Make-ahead* ★ *Festive*

Caramels

MAKES ABOUT 30

BASIC RECIPE

1 CUP (200 G) HEAVY CREAM   1 CUP (200 G) SUGAR
1 TBSP HONEY   SEEDS OF ½ VANILLA BEAN

Line a rectangular dish with parchment paper.
Place the cream and sugar in a large, heavy saucepan,
and stir to combine. Bring to a boil, then reduce
the heat slightly. Stirring constantly, boil until
the mixture is golden-yellow and hard to stir. Stir in
the honey and vanilla seeds. Watch the mixture closely
and don't let it become too dark, otherwise the
caramels will be bitter!

Pour the caramel mixture into the prepared dish
and set in a dry place until cool. Do not refrigerate;
the caramel will absorb humidity and won't harden!
When cool, cut the caramel into small rectangular
candies. Wrap individually in candy wrappers
or parchment paper, or place caramels in an airtight
container. Stored in a cool dry place they will keep
for several months.

TOPPINGS

As the caramel cools in the dish, sprinkle it with any of the following:
chopped (salted) peanuts, finely chopped candied almonds (page 121), fleur de sel,
crushed coffee beans, grated coconut.

Deluxe

FLAVOURINGS

You can further personalize your caramels by folding a flavoring into the mixture before pouring
it into the dish. Try adding one of these ingredients: a pinch of cayenne pepper; ½ teaspoon dark cocoa
powder; ½ teaspoon dried ginger; 1 teaspoon instant coffee powder; ½ teaspoon dried and finely
crushed peppermint leaves; or ½ teaspoon matcha powder. Let your imagination roam free!

HEALTHY ENERGY

HEALTHY ENERGY

A VITAMIN-RICH DIET IS ESPECIALLY IMPORTANT
IN WINTER, AND ENTIRE DAYS OUTDOORS REQUIRE A HEALTHY
NUTRITIONAL MIX TO FILL UP ONE'S BATTERIES FOR THE NEXT DAY.
THE FOLLOWING RECIPES TICK ALL THE BOXES, ALWAYS TURN OUT WELL,
AND MAKE FOR MEMORABLE MEALS IN A WARM HUT, NO LESS.

Roasted vegetables

OVEN-ROASTED VEGETABLES ALWAYS
MAKE ME HAPPY. WHETHER SERVED
AS A COLORFUL SIDE DISH FOR ROAST PORK
OR WILD GAME BURGERS, OR AS
A VEGETARIAN MAIN COURSE, THIS
VEGETABLE MEDLEY IS PERFECTLY SUITED
TO COLD WEATHER. AND TO TOP IT OFF,
IT IS A DELICIOUS WAY TO GET
ALL THE VITAMINS AND MINERAL NUTRIENTS
YOU NEED AFTER A LONG DAY OUTDOORS.

HEALTHY ENERGY

WINTERY
Roasted vegetables
WITH RED BEET AND SQUASH

SERVES 4

½ SMALL SQUASH, SUCH AS BUTTERNUT OR HOKKAIDO
1 RED BEET ½ FENNEL BULB 4 CARROTS
4 SMALL WAXY POTATOES, SUCH AS YUKON GOLD, OR 1 SWEET POTATO
1 PIECE CELERY ROOT OR 1 PARSNIP 3–4 SHALLOTS OR 2 RED ONIONS
2 GARLIC CLOVES 2 HANDFULS FRESH HERBS, SUCH AS THYME AND ROSEMARY
4 TBSP OLIVE OIL COARSE SALT AND BLACK PEPPER 1 TSP CORIANDER SEEDS
FRESH RED CHILI PEPPERS (OPTIONAL) HANDFUL OF CHOPPED PARSLEY

Preheat a convection oven to 375 °F (190 °C). Peel the first 6 ingredients,
trim and seed if needed, and cut into 1-inch wedges or cubes. Peel the shallots or onions
and slice them in half lengthwise. Smash the garlic with a knife. Pluck the thyme and/or
rosemary leaves from the sprigs. Place all ingredients in a roasting pan or wide baking dish.
Toss with the olive oil and let stand briefly for the flavors to meld. Season with salt and pepper, add the
coriander seeds (crush them lightly, if desired), and combine. For a bit of kick, add some thinly
sliced chili pepper. Transfer pan to the oven. Bake for 35–40 minutes, until vegetables are light golden
brown and tender. Just before serving, garnish with chopped parsley.

VARIATION WITH FRESH GOAT CHEESE
This version is superb as a stand-alone vegetarian dish!

After tossing the vegetables with the olive oil and herbs, add a bit of honey and season with
ras el hanout or turmeric. Let stand briefly. Ten minutes before the vegetables are done, sprinkle them
with chopped walnuts, organic lemon or lime zest, and small chunks of fresh goat cheese from a log.

Winter salad
WITH ORANGES AND NUTS

THIS IS A FABULOUS, QUICKLY ASSEMBLED WINTER SALAD
LOADED WITH VITAMINS. TO TURN IT INTO A VEGETARIAN MAIN COURSE,
TOP WITH FRIED GOAT CHEESE OR HALLOUMI.

SERVES 2

1 BELGIAN ENDIVE   HANDFUL OF RADICCHIO LEAVES
2 HANDFULS LAMB'S LETTUCE LEAVES (MÂCHE)   2 SMALL ORANGES
4 TBSP COARSELY CHOPPED WALNUTS

DRESSING:
½ TSP BROWN SUGAR   2 TBSP WHITE VINEGAR   2 TBSP ORANGE JUICE
2 TBSP OLIVE OIL   SALT AND BLACK PEPPER   PINCH OF TURMERIC

TOPPING (OPTIONAL):
2 TBSP TOASTED PUMPKIN SEEDS (PEPITAS)
2 TBSP DRIED CRANBERRIES

Cut the endive and radicchio leaves into thin strips. Wash well along with the lamb's lettuce, and drain in a colander. Using a paring knife, peel the oranges and dice the flesh. Collect the juice in a bowl to use for the dressing. To make the dressing, place all the ingredients in a screw-top jar, seal, and shake.

Transfer all salad ingredients except walnuts to a bowl, add the dressing, and toss. Divide the salad among deep plates or bowls. Sprinkle with the walnuts. If desired, top with pepitas and dried cranberries.

HEALTHY ENERGY

Lamb's lettuce
WITH BACON

SERVES 2

1 THICK SLICE (ABOUT 3 OZ/80 G) SMOKED BACON   1 SMALL ONION
½ TSP MUSTARD   4–6 TBSP WHITE VINEGAR
1 TSP MAPLE SYRUP OR BROWN SUGAR   SALT AND BLACK PEPPER
4 TBSP OLIVE OIL   1 BUNCH CHIVES, CHOPPED
3–4 HANDFULS LAMB'S LETTUCE LEAVES (MÂCHE)
1 BELGIAN ENDIVE   ½ PEAR

Finely dice the bacon. Place it in a frying pan and fry until crispy. Peel and finely dice the onion, add it to the pan with the bacon, and sauté until soft and translucent. Place the bacon and onions in a small bowl or screw-top jar, add the mustard, vinegar, maple syrup or sugar, salt, and pepper. Stir in the oil a little bit at a time, or add it to the jar and shake well. Taste and adjust seasonings. Stir in the chives.

Wash the lamb's lettuce well until the water runs clear. Wash the endive in warm water and cut into strips. Core and thinly slice the pear. Transfer the greens to a mixing bowl, add the dressing, and toss. Divide among deep plates. Garnish with the pear slices.

If desired, toasted seeds and nuts or sprouts make excellent toppings for the salad.

LUXURY VERSION
Enrich the dressing by adding 1 tablespoon of cranberries, then top the salad with thin slices of smoked venison ham or smoked duck breast.

Pan-fried fish fillets

OVER BALSAMIC LENTILS

2 CARROTS	2 CUPS (500 ML) ORGANIC VEGETABLE STOCK
2 STALKS CELERY	SALT AND BLACK PEPPER
½ ONION OR 1 SHALLOT	1 TBSP BUTTER
1 GARLIC CLOVE	½ BUNCH PARSLEY, CHOPPED
4 TBSP OLIVE OR CANOLA OIL	2 FISH FILLETS, 5 ½ OZ (150 G) EACH, SUCH
1 CUP SMALL RED	AS WALLEYE OR ARCTIC CHAR
OR YELLOW LENTILS	JUICE OF ½ LEMON
5 TBSP BALSAMIC VINEGAR	2 TBSP FLOUR

Peel and finely dice the carrots. Wash and dice the celery. Peel and finely dice the onion or shallot and garlic. Heat 2 tablespoons of the oil in a deep skillet or saucepan. Add the carrots, celery, onion, and garlic, and sauté. Add the lentils and stir. Deglaze with the vinegar, pour in the stock, and bring to a boil. Simmer over medium heat for 15 minutes or until the lentils are tender. Season to taste with salt and pepper. Stir in ½ tablespoon of the butter and the parsley.

While the lentils are cooking, prepare the fish. Pat the fillets dry (do not wash them!). Season them on a plate with the lemon juice, salt, and pepper. Place the flour in a second plate. Dredge the fillets in the flour, shaking off any excess. Heat the remaining 2 tablespoons of oil in a non-stick frying pan. Place the fish fillets in the pan skin-side down (this is important; see Tip below). Reduce the heat. When the tops of the fillets are slightly translucent, flip them over. Add the remaining ½ tablespoon of butter to the frying pan and briefly cook the fillets on the other side.

Arrange the fish on top of the lentils. If you like, serve buttered potatoes on the side.

TIP

Fry the fish fillets skin-side down for the first three-quarters of the cooking time. This makes the skin nice and crispy, and ensures the fish does not dry out. Use a non-stick skillet or frying pan. Reduce the heat by about half after placing the fillets in the hot pan. Watch closely to make sure the skin does not burn.

VEGETARIAN VERSION

For a vegetarian version, simply leave out the fish and add more vegetables to the lentils. Parsnips, leeks, and cherry tomatoes all work well. I like this dish served alongside baby potatoes boiled in their skins, then peeled.

THIS SIMPLE RECIPE TASTES BEST WITH HOMEMADE GNOCCHI,
OF COURSE. WHEN TIME IS SHORT AND A DISH MUST BE MADE QUICKLY,
USE A PACKAGE OF READY-MADE GNOCCHI. IN THIS CASE, OPT FOR FRESH
RATHER THAN DRIED GNOCCHI. TURMERIC, WHEN USED REGULARLY
IN COOKING, GOES BEYOND WONDERFUL FLAVOR AND A BURST
OF COLOR TO STRENGTHEN THE IMMUNE SYSTEM.

Gnocchi
IN A HOKKAIDO SQUASH AND TURMERIC SAUCE

SERVES 2

FOR THE GNOCCHI:
4 – 5 LARGE (7 OZ / 200 G) STARCHY OR WAXY POTATOES
1 CUP (250 G) RICOTTA CHEESE
3 ½ OZ (100 G) PASTRY FLOUR
1 EGG YOLK
SALT, BLACK PEPPER, FRESHLY GRATED NUTMEG
4 TBSP GRATED PARMESAN CHEESE
2 TBSP DRY-TOASTED, FINELY CHOPPED OR GROUND
PUMPKIN SEEDS (PEPITAS)

Boil the potatoes in a pot of salted water for 20 minutes,
or until tender. Drain and peel, then mash the potatoes
and transfer to a plate to let the steam evaporate.
Place the potatoes in a bowl, add all the other ingredients,
and combine to make a dough.

Place the dough on a lightly floured work surface. Roll it out
into ¾-inch (2 cm) thick logs. Using a sharp knife, slice the
logs into ¾-inch (2 cm) pieces. Slide the gnocchi into a pot of
boiling salted water and lower the heat to a bare simmer.
Cook the gnocchi until they float to the surface. Remove from
the pot with a slotted spoon.

FOR THE TURMERIC SAUCE:
½ HOKKAIDO SQUASH
1 SHALLOT
1 GARLIC CLOVE
1 SMALL FRESH RED CHILI PEPPER (OPTIONAL)
2 TBSP OLIVE OIL
1 LADLEFUL WHITE WINE OR STOCK
½ CUP (100 G) HEAVY CREAM
1 TSP TURMERIC
½ BUNCH PARSLEY, CHOPPED
PARMESAN CHEESE, FOR GRATING

Wash the squash and scrape out the seeds with a spoon. Cut the squash into ½-inch (1 ¼ cm) cubes. Peel and finely chop the shallot and garlic. If using the chili pepper, seed and finely chop it. Heat the oil in a deep skillet over medium heat. Add the shallot, garlic, and chili, if using, and sauté. Add the squash, then deglaze with the wine or stock. Add the cream and turmeric and stir. Boil gently until the squash is tender but still has a bite.

Fold the gnocchi gently into the sauce. Season to taste with salt and pepper, then add the chopped parsley. Serve the gnocchi in deep plates topped with freshly grated Parmesan.

★ Quick   ★ Vegetarian   ★ Energy

Barley risotto
WITH DRIED WILD MUSHROOMS

DO YOU LIKE FORAGING FOR MUSHROOMS IN THE FALL? IF SO, HAVE YOU TRIED
DRYING THESE LITTLE TREASURES OF FLAVOR WHEN THEY ARE AT THEIR PEAK FOR EATING
IN WINTER? INSTRUCTIONS ON DRYING MUSHROOMS CAN BE FOUND ON PAGE 18—THOUGH,
OF COURSE, YOU CAN ALSO BUY DRIED MUSHROOMS AT QUALITY FOOD STORES AND
SOME FARMERS' MARKETS. DRIED MUSHROOMS WORK ESPECIALLY WELL WITH THE BARLEY
IN THIS RISOTTO. THEY SIMPLY TASTE DELICIOUS.

INGREDIENTS

SERVES 2

½ CUP DRIED WILD MUSHROOMS
½ MEDIUM ONION OR 1 SHALLOT
1 GARLIC CLOVE
2 TBSP OLIVE OIL
½ CUP (100 G) PEARL BARLEY
½ GLASS WHITE WINE
SALT AND BLACK PEPPER
2 CUPS (500 ML) BEEF, CHICKEN, OR
VEGETABLE STOCK
½ LEMON
1 TBSP BUTTER
1 CUP GRATED PARMESAN OR AGED
GRUYÈRE CHEESE
½ BUNCH PARSLEY, CHOPPED

TIP

If you are serving the risotto as a vegetarian
main course, gently fold in a handful
of coarsely chopped arugula just before
serving. Barley risotto shines just as brightly
as a creamy side for grilled meat, game,
and poultry.

PREPERATION

Soak the mushrooms in 1 cup water for at least 1 hour.
Drain in a fine-mesh sieve set over a bowl to catch
and reserve the soaking water. While the mushrooms
are soaking, peel and finely chop the onion or shallot and
garlic. In a deep skillet, heat the oil. Add the onion
and garlic, and briefly sauté. Add the barley and drained
mushrooms and sweat briefly.

Add the wine and deglaze by scraping up the browned
bits. Lightly season with salt and pepper. Add the stock
bit by bit, making sure it is fully absorbed between
additions. If desired, add some of the soaking water
to enhance the earthy flavor of the mushrooms.
Simmer over medium heat, stirring or shaking the pan
occasionally. Turn off the heat after about 25 minutes.

Remove from heat, cover the skillet, and let the risotto
stand for 5 minutes. Place the skillet on a trivet to
allow the skillet, rather than the surface below, to retain
the stored energy. Wash, zest, and juice the lemon. Stir
the zest and juice into the risotto.

To finish the dish, fold in the butter and the grated
Parmesan or Gruyère. Taste and adjust the salt and
pepper, then garnish with chopped parsley.

I REALLY LIKE USING PICKLED FISH
FILLETS THAT I HAVE MADE MYSELF AT HOME (PAGE 26).
NATURALLY, STORE-BOUGHT PICKLED HERRING
FILLETS CAN BE SUBSTITUTED AND TURNED
INTO AN INTENSELY DELICIOUS, PROTEIN-AND-OMEGA-3-
LADEN DISH TO KEEP YOU GOING.

★ *Quick*   ★ *Deluxe*   ★ *Energy*

Pickled herring
IN A CREAMY SAUCE
WITH BOILED POTATOES

1 WHITE ONION   1 LARGE APPLE   2 DILL PICKLES
4 PICKLED HERRING FILLETS OR OTHER PICKLED FISH FILLETS (PAGE 26)
½ CUP YOGURT   ½ CUP (100 G) FULL-FAT SOUR CREAM
½ LEMON   SALT AND BLACK PEPPER
1 SMALL BUNCH FRESH DILL   ½ CUP (100 G) HEAVY CREAM
4 – 5 LARGE (1 LB 2 OZ / 500 G) POTATOES
BUTTER, FOR THE POTATOES

Peel the onion and slice into rings; set aside some onion rings for garnish.
Cut the apple into 8 wedges, core, and thinly slice it. Dice the pickles.
Drain and halve the fish fillets. Mix together the yogurt and sour cream.
Juice the lemon half. Stir the juice into the yogurt mixture and season
to taste with salt and pepper. Finely chop the dill and stir it in. In a bowl place
the onion rings, apple, pickles, fish, yogurt mixture, and heavy cream,
and stir to combine. Marinate for at least 1 hour in the refrigerator (or outside,
if you are in the mountains and it is cold enough).

About 30 – 45 minutes before you plan on eating, boil the potatoes in
a pot of salted water for about 20 minutes, or until tender. Peel the potatoes
and keep them warm.

Divide the fish among 2 plates. Top with a few onion rings.
Make a slit in each potato, push a pat of butter into it, and serve with the herring.

★ *Vegetarian*

VEGETARIAN VERSION
The fish in this recipe can be replaced with red beets pickled in vinegar
(also delicious). Use beets you have pickled yourself, or store-bought
pickled organic beets from a jar or can. To serve, garnish the beets with
chopped walnuts and substitute parsley for the dill.

*I LOVE MAKING ONE-POT PASTA DISHES, ESPECIALLY WHEN
TIME IS OF THE ESSENCE. THEY ARE QUICK, SATISFYING, AND UNCOMPLICATED.
WHY SPEND PRECIOUS ENERGY MAKING LUNCH IN THE HUT WHEN YOU
CAN SAVE IT FOR THE SNOW INSTEAD?*

SERVES 2

One-pot penne
WITH CHICKEN

*1 SMALL CHICKEN BREAST, ABOUT 7 OZ (200 G)
SALT AND BLACK PEPPER   2 TBSP SOY SAUCE
JUICE OF ½ ORGANIC LEMON   ½ ONION
1–2 GARLIC CLOVES   1 CUP FRESH GREEN BEANS
2 CUPS CHERRY TOMATOES   9 OZ (250 G) PENNE
½ BUNCH PARSLEY, CHOPPED   1 TBSP BUTTER OR OLIVE OIL
GRATED PARMESAN, FOR SERVING*

Season the chicken with the salt, pepper, soy sauce, and lemon juice.
For more color and texture, briefly sear the chicken breast in a skillet, then
(or just before cooking) cut it into ¾-inch (2 cm) pieces. Bring 2 cups (½ l)
of water to a boil, then add salt. While you wait for the water to boil, peel and
finely chop the onion and garlic. Wash the green beans and cherry tomatoes.
Cut the beans into 2 or 3 segments.

When the water comes to a boil, add the penne, chicken pieces, onion,
and garlic to the pot. Stir often to ensure the ingredients don't stick to the bottom.
Halfway through the pasta cooking time (check the package instructions),
add the beans and tomatoes. If needed, add a bit more water. One minute before
the pasta is cooked, stir in the parsley and butter or oil. Season to taste with salt and pepper.
The penne should be al dente and the sauce creamy. Serve with grated Parmesan cheese.

TIP

If the pasta is cooked but the sauce is still too thin, add the Parmesan cheese
directly to the pot and mix well. This should help thicken the sauce.

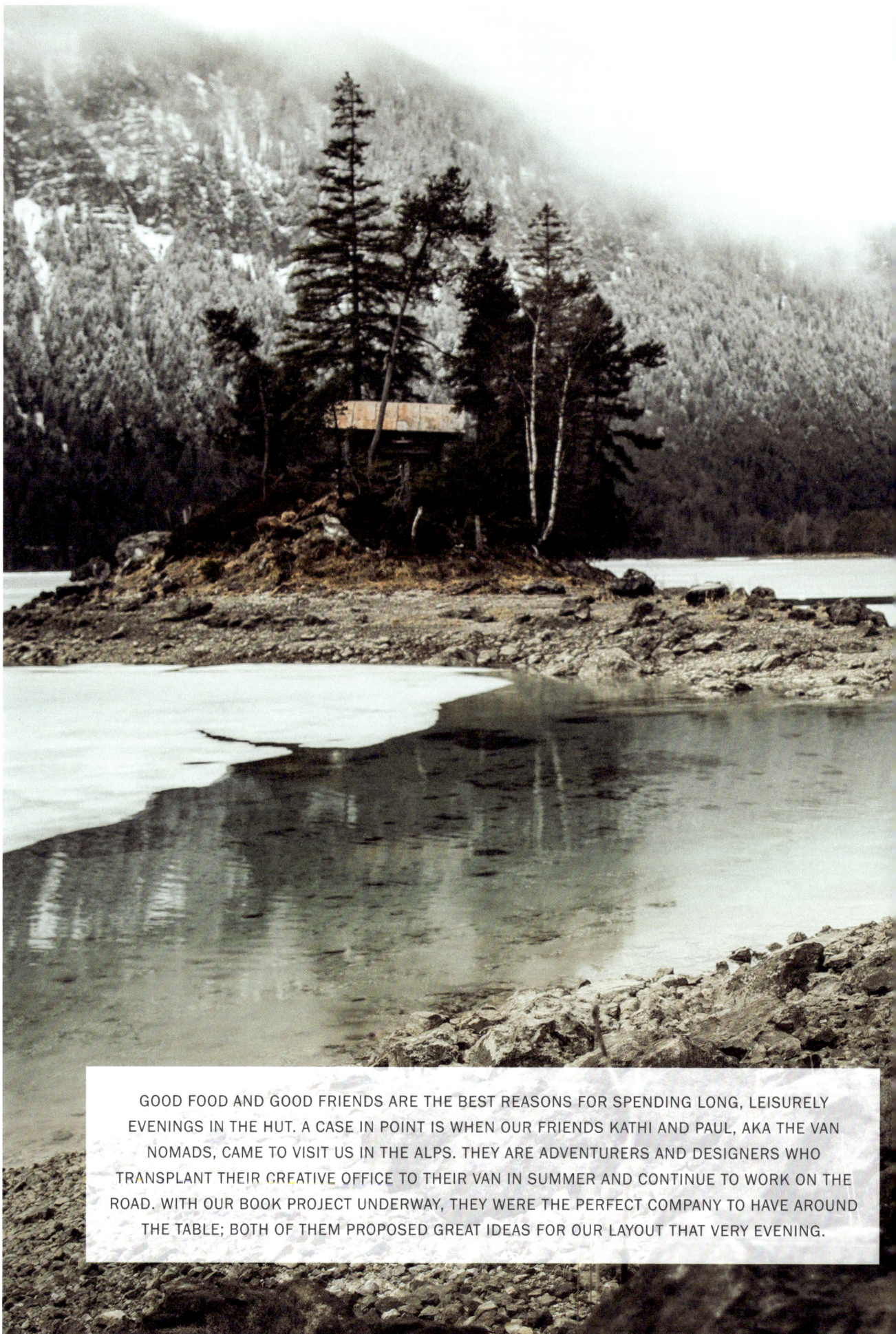

GOOD FOOD AND GOOD FRIENDS ARE THE BEST REASONS FOR SPENDING LONG, LEISURELY EVENINGS IN THE HUT. A CASE IN POINT IS WHEN OUR FRIENDS KATHI AND PAUL, AKA THE VAN NOMADS, CAME TO VISIT US IN THE ALPS. THEY ARE ADVENTURERS AND DESIGNERS WHO TRANSPLANT THEIR CREATIVE OFFICE TO THEIR VAN IN SUMMER AND CONTINUE TO WORK ON THE ROAD. WITH OUR BOOK PROJECT UNDERWAY, THEY WERE THE PERFECT COMPANY TO HAVE AROUND THE TABLE; BOTH OF THEM PROPOSED GREAT IDEAS FOR OUR LAYOUT THAT VERY EVENING.

SIMPLE, STRAIGHTFORWARD, EVEN TRENDY...
HERE'S ANOTHER ONE-POT PASTA DISH TO SAVE THE DAY.
COOKING ALL THE INGREDIENTS IN A SINGLE POT ALLOWS
THE DIFFERENT FLAVORS TO MARRY AND THE PASTA TO
ABSORB THEM ALL. A REAL TASTE EXPLOSION!

SERVES 2

One-pot tagliatelle
WITH SMOKED SALMON

ABOUT 2 CUPS (500 ML) ORGANIC VEGETABLE STOCK
½ ONION   1 GARLIC CLOVE   2–3 SPRING ONIONS OR 1 LEEK
1 SMALL PACKAGE (ABOUT 4 ½ OZ / 125 G) SMOKED SALMON, SEPARATED INTO SLICES
9 OZ (250 G) TAGLIATELLE   ½ CUP (100 G) SOUR CREAM
2 CUPS FRESH SPINACH, WASHED AND DRAINED
1 BUNCH FRESH DILL OR CHIVES, CHOPPED   ZEST AND JUICE OF ½ ORGANIC LEMON
SALT AND BLACK PEPPER

Pour the stock into a pot and bring to a boil. In the meantime,
peel and finely chop the onion and garlic. Trim and slice the spring onions or leek.
Cut the salmon into thin strips. Add the pasta, onion, and garlic to the boiling stock.
Stir now and then so that nothing sticks to the bottom of the pot. Halfway
through the pasta cooking time (check the package instructions), add the sour cream,
spring onions or leek, and spinach. One minute before the pasta is cooked, stir in
the salmon, dill, lemon juice, and lemon zest. Season to taste with salt and pepper.
The tagliatelle should be al dente and the sauce nice and creamy.

WARM
Red beet salad
WITH WALNUTS

A SUPER-DELICIOUS AND HEALTHY WINTER SALAD MADE WITH COOKED RED BEETS, THIS WORKS BOTH AS A FIRST COURSE OR AS A SIDE FOR STEAK, GRILLED CHICKEN, OR WILD GAME. AND NO MATTER HOW YOU SERVE IT, THE DEEP, VIBRANT COLOR OF THIS SALAD IS OH-SO APPEALING.

2 RED BEETS   1 APPLE   4 TBSP RAW WALNUTS
½ TSP BROWN SUGAR   2 TBSP WHITE VINEGAR   2 TBSP SOUR CREAM
2 TBSP OLIVE OIL   SALT AND BLACK PEPPER

HEALTHY ENERGY

Place the beets, unpeeled, in a pot with salted water. Add a splash of white vinegar, bring to a boil, and cook until tender. (You can use a pressure cooker, too.)

Make sure to cut off and reserve the young beet leaves for later. Red beet leaves are very healthy; they contain a higher amount of the same vitamins compared to the beets themselves. For this reason, when the beets you buy still have their leaves, always use them. Wash the leaves and slice them very thinly.

Test the beets with a skewer for doneness. Let them cool a bit. Peel the beets (ideally wearing rubber gloves), then slice or dice them. Wash, core, and grate or very finely chop the apple. In a dry skillet, toast the walnuts. When cool enough to handle, coarsely crush them with your hands. Place the beets, apple, and walnuts in a bowl. Add the sugar, vinegar, sour cream, and olive oil, and toss to combine. Season to taste with salt and black pepper.

TIP

You really must try this: slice or dice the beets more finely, and use the beet salad as a topping for the Wild Game Burger on page 176. Together with a few oven-fresh sweet potato wedges...yummy!

SERVES 2

SOUTH TYROLEAN
Dumpling salad

WINTERTIME IS DUMPLING TIME.
I DISCOVERED THIS DELICIOUS AND FILLING SALAD WHEN I WAS BACKCOUNTRY
SKIING THOUGH A SMALL VALLEY IN SOUTH TYROL.

WE OFTEN HAVE A FEW BREAD DUMPLINGS LEFTOVER FROM OUR SUNDAY ROAST.
WHEN WE DON'T, WHIPPING UP A FRESH BATCH OF DUMPLINGS MADE
FROM DAY-OLD BREAD IS A SMALL PRICE TO PAY FOR CREATING THIS FABULOUS SALAD.
YOU WILL FIND THE BASIC RECIPE FOR BREAD DUMPLINGS ON PAGE 214.

WHEN USING THEM IN THE SALAD,
ALLOW THE COOKED DUMPLINGS TO COOL A BIT.

HEALTHY ENERGY

2–3 BREAD OR SPINACH DUMPLINGS   2 TBSP BUTTER
2 HANDFULS ARUGULA   2 HANDFULS BITTER SALAD GREENS, SUCH AS BELGIAN ENDIVE,
RADICCHIO, OR OAK LEAF   3 TBSP WHITE BALSAMIC VINEGAR   2 TBSP OLIVE OIL
SALT AND BLACK PEPPER   ½ TSP HOT MUSTARD, SUCH AS DIJON   ½ TSP SUGAR
½ BUNCH CHIVES, CHOPPED   1 PIECE OF FRESH PARMESAN CHEESE (OPTIONAL)
TOASTED PINE NUTS OR PUMPKIN SEEDS, FOR GARNISH

Slice the dumplings. Melt the butter in a frying pan and add the
sliced dumplings. Fry until they are light golden brown. Remove pan from heat and set aside.
Wash and spin dry or drain the salad greens, then mix them together in a bowl.
To make the dressing, place the vinegar, oil, salt, pepper, mustard, sugar, and chives in a screw-top
jar. Cover and shake well. Pour the dressing over the salad and toss. Let stand for
a few minutes to allow flavors to combine. Divide the salad among plates and arrange the warm
dumpling slices on top. If using, shave some Parmesan over the dumplings. If desired,
garnish the salad with a few toasted pine nuts or pumpkin seeds.

A TAGINE IS A CONICAL
CERAMIC BAKING DISH FROM MOROCCO USED TO
SLOWLY BRAISE WONDERFUL STEWS THAT REMAIN MOIST.
THE STEWS THEMSELVES ARE ALSO CALLED TAGINES.
IF YOU DO NOT HAVE A TAGINE, USE A GOOD OLD RÖMERTOPF
(A CLAY ROASTING POT), A DUTCH OVEN, OR ANOTHER KIND
OF HEAVY LIDDED POT. I LEARNED TO LOVE FLAVOR-PACKED TAGINES
ON MY SURFING TRIPS TO MOROCCO. WHETHER IT'S MEAT,
FISH, OR JUST VEGETABLES ON THEIR OWN, EVERYTHING BRAISED
IN A TAGINE TASTES INCREDIBLE AND NEVER LOSES ITS MOISTURE.

Chicken tagine

WITH PRESERVED LEMON

SERVES 2

INGREDIENTS

1 WHITE OR RED ONION   1–2 GARLIC CLOVES
1 SMALL RED CHILI PEPPER (OPTIONAL)   4 TBSP OLIVE OIL
JUICE OF ½ LEMON   SALT AND BLACK PEPPER
1 TSP RAS EL HANOUT OR ½ TSP GROUND CUMIN
½ TSP HUNGARIAN PAPRIKA
FRESH HERBS (IDEALLY CILANTRO AND/OR PARSLEY)
2 CHICKEN LEGS (THIGH AND DRUMSTICK)
1 BELL PEPPER   1 SMALL ZUCCHINI
2 WAXY POTATOES, SUCH AS YUKON GOLD
3 FRESH RIPE TOMATOES OR 8 OZ (225 G)
CANNED DICED TOMATOES
½ PRESERVED LEMON (PAGE 25),
CUT INTO SMALL DICE

PREPERATION

First, make the chermoula (the spiced marinade for the chicken): peel the onion, cut it in half, and finely dice one half. Set the other half aside. Place the diced onion in a bowl. Peel and finely chop the garlic and the chili pepper, if using, and add to the bowl. Add 3 tablespoons of the olive oil and the lemon juice, and stir to combine. Generously season the chermoula with salt, pepper, ras el hanout or cumin, and paprika, and mix well. Chop some of the herbs and add them to the bowl, reserving some whole sprigs for later. Add the chicken legs and mix thoroughly to coat with the chermoula. Refrigerate for at least 1–2 hours.

Wash the bell pepper and zucchini, peel the potatoes, and cut everything into uniform slices or strips about ½-inch (1 ¼ cm) thick. Slice the remaining onion half into rings. Arrange the onion and the remaining tablespoon of olive oil on the bottom of the pot or tagine. Layer the potatoes and vegetables on top, then add the marinated chicken legs, reserving the marinade. Finely chop the tomatoes and place them in a bowl. Add the reserved chermoula and about ½ cup of water to the bowl, and stir to combine. Season with salt and pepper, then pour over the tagine.

Cover pot and place in a cold oven. Set at 400 °F (200 °C) and cook for about 1 ½ hours. Remove from the oven. (If cooking in a tagine, be careful: it will be very hot!) Remove the chicken legs and mix the preserved lemon dice into the vegetables. Arrange the reserved cilantro and parsley sprigs over the vegetables. Place the chicken legs over the herbs. Return the pot to the oven, uncovered. Cook for 15 minutes more, or until the chicken is nicely golden brown and crispy. If you are using fish, vegetables, or lamb (see Tip), skip this last step.

Serve the dish straight from the tagine or Römertopf; this keeps it nice and hot. Traditionally, tagines are served with pita bread. A recipe for pita bread can be found on page 67.

TIP

Depending on what you like and what is available, you could switch up the ingredients in the tagine. Lamb or fish tastes wonderful. Even with just vegetables, a tagine is always flavorful and succulent. When using soft vegetables, keep in mind how long they take to cook and adjust the sizes of the vegetable pieces accordingly.

Traditionally, a tagine is used over a small charcoal stove. You could also use it over a wood fire, in a wood-burning oven, or on a gas ring. If you use a gas ring, make sure to heat the tagine slowly so it doesn't crack. Unglazed tagines should be soaked in water before using them.

HEALTHY ENERGY

Red cabbage salad
WITH FENNEL AND BLOOD ORANGE

THIS DELICIOUS WINTER SALAD IS A COMPLETE WINNER. COUPLED WITH
FANTASTIC FLAVOR IS ITS HIGH NUTRITIONAL VALUE: IT IS ESPECIALLY RICH IN
VITAMIN C AND CAN HELP TO WARD OFF COLDS.

SERVES 2

½ SMALL RED CABBAGE
1 FENNEL BULB
SALT AND BLACK PEPPER
6–8 TBSP WHITE VINEGAR
1–2 BLOOD ORANGES
1 SMALL APPLE
1 TBSP MAPLE SYRUP OR
BROWN SUGAR
4 TBSP OLIVE OIL
2 TBSP COARSELY CHOPPED WALNUTS
3 ½ OZ (100 G) FETA CHEESE OR
4 SLICES FRESH GOAT CHEESE FROM
A LOG (OPTIONAL)

Cut the cabbage in half, remove the core, then cut into
quarters. Thinly slice or shred the cabbage. Since
red cabbage stains, I'd recommend wearing rubber gloves
and using a smooth plastic cutting board when you
handle it (you can also use a mandoline slicer or a food
processor fitted with the shredding disc). Cut the fennel
into quarters, remove the core, and very thinly slice it.
Place the cabbage and fennel in a large bowl and mix them
together. Season generously with salt and pepper. Add the
vinegar. Using your hands, best with rubber gloves, knead
vigorously for about 5 minutes.

With a paring knife, peel the blood oranges and dice
the flesh. Wash, quarter, core, and finely dice the apple.
Add the orange, apple, maple syrup or sugar, and olive
oil to the salad, and toss. Taste and adjust the seasonings.
Ideally, let the salad stand for about 30 minutes before
serving. To serve, sprinkle with the walnuts and cheese,
if using. The salad pairs nicely with grilled meat.

TIP

This salad also tastes unbelievably good in a sandwich made with crusty, rustic bread.
When using in sandwiches I omit the cheese. Slice a crusty bun or small baguette in half, generously
top it with the salad, then add thin slices of grilled meat (such as beef, pork, or game). Season with pepper.
If desired, spread a teaspoon of cranberry jam on the top half of the bread. If the sandwich is going
in your backpack, fill the bun only with meat and pack the salad and any condiments separately.
Because nobody loves soggy bread.

IN THIS CURRY RECIPE, FRESH GINGER AND THE HEAT FROM CHILI SAUCE MAKE IT A COMFORT
DISH OF SORTS THAT WARMS YOU ON THE INSIDE—A FEELING MUCH WELCOME IN WINTERTIME. YOUR IMMUNE
SYSTEM WILL ALSO WELCOME THE TURMERIC AND OTHER VITAMIN-RICH, IMMUNE-BOOSTING INGREDIENTS.

WARMING
Winter curry
WITH YELLOW RICE

SERVES 2

½ HOKKAIDO SQUASH   2 CARROTS   1 SWEET POTATO
½ PARSNIP   1 CHICKEN BREAST (CAN BE REPLACED WITH
EXTRA VEGETABLES OR 7 OZ/200 G TOFU)
1 TBSP SOY SAUCE   1 TSP HONEY   2 TBSP FRESH LIME JUICE
SALT AND BLACK PEPPER   1 MEDIUM ONION
1–2 GARLIC CLOVES   2 TBSP CANOLA OIL
3 TBSP RED CURRY PASTE (PAGE 23)   1 ¾ CUPS (400 ML) COCONUT MILK
½ BUNCH CILANTRO, CHOPPED

THAI SAUCE (OPTIONAL) 1 TSP PALM SUGAR OR BROWN SUGAR
½ TSP FISH SAUCE   2 TBSP FRESH LIME JUICE

RICE: 1 CUP (7 OZ/200 G) BASMATI RICE OR JASMINE RICE
½ TSP TURMERIC

Seed and slice the squash. Peel the carrots, sweet potato, and parsnip.
Cut the vegetables into pieces according to their cooking times. For example, cut the carrots
into smaller pieces than the squash. Cut the chicken breast or tofu into cubes and place in a bowl.
Add the soy sauce, honey, lime juice, salt, and pepper, combine well, and let marinate.

Peel and chop the onion and garlic. Heat the oil in a wok, pot, or large frying pan.
Add the meat or tofu, onions, and garlic, and fry. Add the curry paste, squash, carrots, sweet
potato, and parsnip. Stir-fry briefly. Deglaze with the coconut milk, adding a bit of water or vegetable stock, if needed. Gently simmer the curry for 10–15 minutes. Stir in the Thai sauce,
if using, and season to taste with salt and pepper.

Rinse the rice in cold water. Place it in a saucepan, add the recommended quantity
of water (usually 1 ½ or 2 times the amount of water to rice), a bit of salt, and the turmeric.
Bring to a boil and reduce the heat to low. Cover the saucepan with a tight-fitting lid and cook
the rice for about 10 minutes. Divide the rice among bowls or deep plates and ladle
the curry over the top. Sprinkle with cilantro.

EXPERT TIP

The piperine contained in black pepper greatly
boosts the health-promoting effects of the curcumin
contained in turmeric.

LONG WINTER EVENINGS

OUTSIDE, IT IS BITTERLY COLD. BUT THROUGH THE FROST
ON THE WINDOWS, YOU CAN SEE THE WARM GLOW OF A CRACKLING
FIRE IN THE INVITING LIVING ROOM OF THE MOUNTAIN HUT.
THE AROMA OF PORK ROASTING IN THE WOOD OVEN COMBINED WITH
THE COZY EMBRACE OF THE FIREPLACE SETS THE STAGE FOR THE
EVENING TO COME. NOW IS THE TIME FOR GENUINE "SLOW FOOD."
THE SHORT DAYS AND LONG EVENINGS ARE IDEALLY SUITED TO TACKLING
SLIGHTLY MORE ELABORATE RECIPES. ENJOYMENT IS GUARANTEED!

AS YOU MIGHT EXPECT, BURGERS TASTE REALLY GOOD IN WINTER. AND IF YOU CAN GET
WILD GAME, YOU WILL ADD A TRULY AMAZING DIMENSION OF FLAVOR TO YOUR BURGERS.
HIGH-QUALITY INGREDIENTS, SPECIAL CHEESE, AND YOUR OWN CREATIVITY ARE
ENOUGH TO TURN THE HUMBLE BURGER INTO A VERITABLE HIGHLIGHT. MAKING BURGER
BUNS FROM SCRATCH ALSO MAKES A HUGE DIFFERENCE. IF THE GAME MEAT IS
VERY FRESH YOU CAN SERVE THE PATTIES MEDIUM-RARE. SINCE VENISON IS RELATIVELY LEAN,
MIX IT UP WITH A BIT OF FATTY GROUND GAME MEAT, IF POSSIBLE, SUCH AS WILD BOAR
OR ALPINE IBEX (CHAMOIS) MEAT. IF ALL ELSE FAILS, REGULAR GROUND PORK WILL ALSO DO.

Deluxe *Wood stove*

Wild game burgers

WITH SWEET POTATO WEDGES

YELLOW BURGER BUNS

MAKES 4-6 BUNS

½ CUP (125 ML) WARM MILK   1 TBSP SUGAR   ½ OZ (14 G) FRESH YEAST OR 1 ¼ TSP ACTIVE DRY YEAST
¾ OZ (20 G) MELTED BUTTER   9 OZ (250 G) ALL-PURPOSE FLOUR OR LIGHT SPELT FLOUR
½ TSP SALT   ½ TSP TURMERIC   1 TSP CHOPPED THYME   1 TSP CHOPPED ROSEMARY
2 EGGS AT ROOM TEMPERATURE   MIX OF 1 TSP GROUND CORIANDER
½ TSP TOASTED AND CRUSHED ALLSPICE   1 TSP SESAME SEEDS

To make the starter, stir together the warm milk, sugar, yeast, and butter. Cover and let stand until
the liquid foams slightly. Combine the flour, salt, turmeric, thyme, and rosemary in a bowl. Add 1 egg and the starter.
Knead the dough vigorously. If the dough is too sticky, work in a bit more flour; if it is too firm,
work in some milk. Cover the dough and let it rise for 1 hour. Briefly knead the dough again to remove air bubbles.
Shape the dough into 6 flat buns. Cover and let rise for 30 minutes more.

Preheat the oven to 375 °F (190 °C). Beat the remaining egg with a bit of water. Brush the egg
mixture over the buns and sprinkle with the spice and seed mix. Bake for 20 minutes or until golden brown.
Remove from the oven and cover the buns with a kitchen towel to keep them soft as they cool.
Use the buns right away, or freeze them in freezer bags.

WILD GAME BURGERS

MAKES 2 BURGERS

*10 OZ (300 G) GROUND GAME MEAT (FOR EXAMPLE 70% VENISON, 30% WILD BOAR)
½ TSP EACH SALT AND BLACK PEPPER   1 DILL PICKLE   1 RIPE BEEFSTEAK TOMATO
4 SLICES BACON   1 RED ONION   1 TBSP BALSAMIC VINEGAR   2 TSP BARBECUE SAUCE
2 TSP CRANBERRIES FROM A JAR   2 SLICES SOFT CHEESE, SUCH AS TALEGGIO
OR BLUE CHEESE   1 HANDFUL WILD HERBS   2 TSP FIG MUSTARD (PAGE 30)*

OPTIONAL: *FRESH GARDEN CRESS OR SPROUTS*

Preheat the barbecue. Season the meat with salt and pepper and knead well. Moisten your
hands and shape the meat into 2 patties slightly bigger than the size of a bun, since they
will shrink a bit when they cook. Slice the pickle and tomato. Place the bacon in a frying pan and fry
until crisp. Remove bacon from the pan and set aside, reserving the fat. Slice the onion into thin rings and
sauté in the bacon fat until soft and translucent. Deglaze with the vinegar and cook until the sauce
reduces. In a small bowl, stir together the barbecue sauce and the cranberries.

Grill the burgers on one side, flip them over, and top the grilled side with the cheese.
Slice the buns in half and lightly toast them on the grill, cut-side down.

Arrange all the ingredients on the bottom halves of the buns. Before topping each burger with
the other half of the bun, add the garden cress and sprouts, if using.

SWEET POTATO WEDGES

*3 - 4 LARGE SWEET POTATOES
3 - 4 TBSP OLIVE OIL
COARSE SEA SALT, SUCH AS FLEUR DE SEL*

Sweet potato wedges are a natural pairing for the burgers. To make them, preheat
the oven to 400 °F (200 °C). Peel the sweet potatoes and cut them into ½-inch (1 ¼ cm) slices.
In a large bowl, toss the potatoes with the olive oil and salt. Transfer to a baking tray.
Bake for 30 minutes or until tender and golden brown.

LONG WINTER EVENINGS

Roast pork

THIS SUCCULENT ROAST WITH ITS CRISPY
CRACKLING IS FOOLPROOF. IS IT APPROPRIATE FOR
A LEISURELY EVENING IN A MOUNTAIN HUT?
ABSOLUTELY, AND IT IS SURE TO DELIGHT YOUR
GUESTS! IDEALLY SERVED WITH THE ROASTED
VEGETABLES ON PAGES 136 – 139, YOU CAN POP THE
VEGGIES IN THE OVEN ALONG WITH THE MEAT
DURING THE LAST 45 MINUTES OF COOKING TIME.
THIS MEANS NO STRESS IN THE KITCHEN.
THE TRADITIONAL VERSION WITH CARAWAY SEEDS
IS SERVED WITH POTATOES OR BREAD DUMPLINGS
(PAGE 214) AND BLAUKRAUT (PAGE 29). IF YOU
ARE USING A WOOD-BURNING OVEN, MAKE SURE IT
DOESN'T GET TOO HOT. THE SLOWER THE ROAST
COOKS THE JUICIER IT WILL BE.

TIP

If you have a great deal of time and want to serve genuine slow food, cook the pork low and slow. After searing the meat, cook it in the oven for about 4 hours at 175 °F (80 °C). During the last 20 minutes of cooking time, raise the heat to 325–360 °F (160–180 °C). This ensures the crackling will be nice and crisp, while the meat remains especially juicy and tender. The winter spice mix adds an extra layer of flavor, and the roast goes beyond a good meal to become an experience with special flair.

Roast pork
WITH DARK BEER GRAVY

SERVES 4–6

INGREDIENTS

1 LB 2 OZ (500 G) MIXED VEGETABLES FOR ROASTING
(SUCH AS CARROTS, CELERY ROOT, ONIONS, AND PARSNIPS)
2 GARLIC CLOVES
3 LB 3 OZ (1.5 KG) SKIN-ON PORK, SUCH AS PORK SHOULDER,
FROM A HUMANELY RAISED PIG OR A WILD BOAR
SALT   BLACK PEPPER   HUNGARIAN PAPRIKA
1 TBSP MUSTARD
2 TBSP VEGETABLE OIL, FOR FRYING
10 OZ (300 G) PORK BONES (OR BACK RIBS, WHOLE
OR CUT INTO INDIVIDUAL RIBS)
1–2 TBSP FLOUR
1 TBSP TOMATO PASTE
2 CUPS (500 ML) BEEF STOCK OR WATER
2 CUPS (500 ML) DARK BEER

WINTER SPICE MIX:
½ TSP JUNIPER BERRIES   ½ TSP ALLSPICE
2–3 WHOLE CLOVES   PINCH OF CINNAMON
1 ORGANIC ORANGE, DICED
1 TBSP HONEY

LONG WINTER EVENINGS

TIP

When I make traditional pork roast, I use ½ tsp whole caraway
seeds instead of the winter spice mix.

PREPERATION

Preheat a convection oven to 325 °F (160 °C) or fire up the wood oven. Peel the onions, wash the other vegetables, and coarsely dice them. Smash the unpeeled garlic. Generously season the pork with salt, pepper, and paprika. Spread the mustard over the pork and score the skin. Heat the oil in a roasting pan and sear the pork and the bones or ribs on all sides in the oil. Remove from the pan and set aside. Place the onions, garlic, and the rest of the vegetables in the roasting pan and fry them in the remaining fat until golden brown. Dust with flour, then add the tomato paste and winter spice mix. Pour in the stock or water.

Place the pork, skin-side down, on top of the vegetables. Deglaze with a bit of the beer. Transfer the roasting pan to the oven and cook for 1 hour. Now and then, pour a bit of beer into the pan. After an hour, turn the pork skin-side up. Roast for 1 hour more. Gradually pour the remaining beer into the pan bit by bit. Increase the heat and cook for 10 minutes more, until the skin is nicely browned and crisp. If the skin is dark enough, cover the pork with aluminum foil. Remove the roast and the ribs (which will taste fabulous, too) from the roasting pan and keep warm.

To make the gravy, pour the pan juices, the vegetables, and the bones (if you used them instead of ribs) through a large sieve into a saucepan. Bring to a boil and reduce. Season to taste with salt and pepper. Carve the pork into thin slices and serve with the gravy.

LONG WINTER EVENINGS

SERVES 4

Hearty goulash

5 LARGE WHITE ONIONS   1 CARROT   2–3 GARLIC CLOVES   2.2 LB (1 KG) STEWING BEEF
SALT AND BLACK PEPPER   2 TBSP VEGETABLE OIL (FOR FRYING) OR CLARIFIED BUTTER
2–3 TBSP TOMATO PASTE   1 ½ CUPS (375 ML) RED WINE
FOR THE GOULASH SPICE MIX: 1 TSP EACH HOT AND SWEET HUNGARIAN PAPRIKA
1 TSP CRUSHED CARAWAY SEEDS   ½ TSP CANE SUGAR
1 TBSP FLOUR   2 CUPS (500 ML) BEEF STOCK (PAGE 188)   2–3 BAY LEAVES
½ BUNCH PARSLEY, CHOPPED

Peel the onions and cut them into rings or thin slices. Peel and finely dice the carrot.
Peel and finely chop the garlic. Season the beef with salt and pepper. Heat the oil in a Dutch oven
or large pot. Working in batches, brown the meat on all sides in the oil or butter. Remove and
set aside. Add the onion to the pot and sauté until soft and translucent. Add the tomato paste, then
a bit of the wine. Deglaze by scraping up the brown bits from the bottom of the pot. Repeat
2 or 3 more times with the rest of the wine. The last time, add the spice mix and the flour. Return the
meat to the pot. Add stock, bay leaves, and carrot, season with salt and pepper, and stir well.
Bring to a boil. Reduce heat to low, cover, and simmer for 1 ½–2 hours; 20 minutes before the end
of cooking time, stir garlic into the goulash.

Before serving, garnish with chopped parsley. Serve with Bread Dumplings (page 214),
egg noodles, savory polenta, spätzle noodles, rice, or bread.

TIP

If you are pressed for time, you can cook the goulash in a pressure cooker.
Just reduce the cooking time by about 1 hour.
Leftover goulash makes a great dish to bring along with you in a thermos.

VARIATION SZEGEDIN GOULASH

8 OZ (225 G) CANNED SAUERKRAUT, DRAINED   ½ CUP SOUR CREAM

Prepare the goulash as described above.
Halfway through the cooking time, add the sauerkraut. Stir in the sour cream before serving.

A HEARTY STOCK IS THE BASIS OF MANY SOUPS AND SAUCES. RICH AND FLAVORFUL, IT SUPPLIES YOUR BODY WITH HEALTHY FUEL AND ENERGY. IT WILL ONLY TAKE ONE SPOONFUL OF HOMEMADE STOCK TO MAKE YOU A DEVOTEE; THERE WILL BE NO NEED FOR ME TO FURTHER EXPLAIN THE DIFFERENCE IN FLAVOR BETWEEN HOMEMADE AND STORE-BOUGHT STOCK, NOT TO MENTION THAT THE HOMEMADE STUFF IS ALSO FREE FROM TASTE ENHANCERS AND OTHER UNDESIRABLE INGREDIENTS. I ALWAYS USE ORGANIC VEGETABLES, PRIMARILY FROM LOCAL FARMERS I CAN TRUST. THIS IS VERY IMPORTANT TO ME. STOCK FREEZES WELL, SO IT CAN BE MADE AHEAD OF TIME AND FROZEN IN SMALL PORTIONS. THIS WAY YOU HAVE STOCK ON HAND WHEN YOU NEED IT, AND ONE LESS REASON TO STRESS.

Beef stock

MAKES 8 CUPS (2 LITERS)

1 LB 2 OZ (500 G) BEEF BONES, CUT INTO SMALLER PIECES
2.2 LB (1 KG) BEEF (CHUCK OR SHOULDER)
WHOLE PEPPERCORNS   ALLSPICE BERRIES   MUSTARD SEEDS   CORIANDER SEEDS (A FEW OF EACH)
1–2 BAY LEAVES   3–4 CARROTS   ½ LEEK   ¼ CELERY ROOT OR 4 CELERY STALKS
1–2 GARLIC CLOVES   1–2 ONIONS   BUNCH OF PARSLEY   1 TSP SALT

Wash the bones in cold water. Place the bones and the meat in a large stockpot. Add 8 cups (2 l) of cold water and bring to a boil. Add the spices and return soup to a boil. Reduce heat and simmer gently for about 1 hour. Using a slotted spoon, skim off the foam (which is coagulated protein). Wash and roughly chop the vegetables. Peel and halve the garlic cloves.

Cut the unpeeled onions in half. Place them in a skillet cut-side down or directly on the hot top of a wood stove until charred. This will give the stock a deeper color. Add the vegetables, garlic, onions, and parsley sprigs to the stockpot.

Simmer the stock for another hour. Now and then, test the beef with a fork. When the fork comes out easily and the juices run clear, the beef is cooked. Remove beef from the pot; if you intend to eat it right away, keep warm. If not, in a bowl dissolve 1 teaspoon of salt in cold water and place the beef in the water. Season the stock with salt. Place a large strainer over a large bowl and strain the stock.

TIP

For a slightly fancier stock you can use veal chuck or shoulder and veal bones instead of beef. To make a very clear stock, let it cool after straining, then pour it into a clean pot. Mix about 10 oz (300 g) ground beef with 1 or 2 egg whites and finely diced root vegetables, and add it to the stock. Slowly bring the stock to a boil without stirring. This clarifies the stock and gives it a more concentrated, richer flavor. Strain the stock into a large bowl, and voilà!

LONG WINTER EVENINGS

I AM OFTEN ASKED TO NAME MY FAVORITE MEAL. THIS WONDERFULLY JUICY BEEF DISH MOST DEFINITELY TOPS THE LIST: IT IS CLASSIC, VERY HEALTHY, AND, WHEN FRESHLY PREPARED, AN EXAMPLE OF PERFECT HARMONY BETWEEN INGREDIENTS.

Poached beef
WITH ROOT VEGETABLES

SERVES 4

2.2 LB (1 KG) WAXY POTATOES
2.2 LB (1 KG) POACHED BEEF
(SEE BEEF STOCK RECIPE, PAGE 188)
1 SHALLOT   2 TBSP BUTTER
2 TBSP FLOUR
1 – 2 LADLEFULS BEEF STOCK (PAGE 188)
½ CUP HEAVY CREAM
½ HORSERADISH ROOT
SALT   FRESHLY GRATED NUTMEG
2 CARROTS
½ LEEK   ¼ CELERY ROOT
1 BUNCH CHIVES

Boil the potatoes in a pot of salted water for 20 minutes or until tender. Peel and keep warm. Cut the beef into thin slices. If needed, heat the beef slices gently in a bit of stock or salted water.

Peel and finely chop the shallot. Melt 1 tablespoon of the butter in a small saucepan. Add the shallot, sauté until soft and translucent, then dust with the flour. Deglaze with the stock and stir in the cream. Grate the horseradish into the sauce, reserving some for garnish. (For a smoother sauce, purée briefly with an immersion blender.) Season to taste with salt and nutmeg.

Wash and peel the carrots, leek, and celery root. Cut into 2-inch (5 cm) strips. Heat the remaining tablespoon of butter in a skillet. Add the vegetables. Season with salt, add a splash of water, and cook briefly. Finely chop the chives.

Warm 4 plates. Arrange slices of beef in the center of each plate. Ladle the horseradish sauce over the meat. Place a few potatoes around it, and top the meat with vegetables. Garnish with a sprinkle of freshly grated horseradish and chopped chives.

★ Deluxe   ★ Energy

★ Quick ★ Energy

THIS MOUTHWATERING HASH MAKES A TRULY HEARTY FEAST,
AND IT IS A GREAT WAY TO USE UP LEFTOVERS. ALL YOU NEED IS A THICK SLICE
OF FRAGRANT FARMER'S BREAD WITH BUTTER FOR ULTIMATE PERFECTION.

Tyrolean hash

WITH POACHED BEEF AND GREEN BEANS

SERVES 2

INGREDIENTS

4 SLICES POACHED BEEF (SEE BEEF STOCK RECIPE, PAGE 188)
4 COOKED MEDIUM POTATOES (OR LEFTOVERS FROM THE PREVIOUS DAY)
2 TBSP OLIVE OIL   1 WHITE OR RED ONION
½ TSP CARAWAY SEEDS   HANDFUL OF GREEN BEANS
½ TBSP BUTTER   2–4 EGGS   SALT AND BLACK PEPPER
½ BUNCH PARSLEY OR CHIVES   ½ TSP DRIED OREGANO (OPTIONAL)

PREPERATION

Cut the slices of beef into diamond shapes. Peel and slice the potatoes. Heat the oil in a cast-iron
skillet or frying pan. Add the potatoes and fry until golden brown. Meanwhile peel and dice the onion.
Add the onion and caraway seeds to the skillet and fry along with the potatoes. Slice the beans
(if desired, blanch them first). Add the beef, beans, and butter to the skillet.

Beat the eggs and pour them into the skillet; alternatively, you can beat and cook the eggs in a separate skillet.
Season the hash with salt and pepper, and garnish with plenty of chopped herbs and dried oregano, if desired.
The hash tastes best served straight from the cast-iron skillet, so everyone can help themselves.

VEGETARIAN VERSION
Use more green vegetables, such as green asparagus,
leek, or broccoli instead of beef.

Roast chicken

WITH WINTER SPICES BAKED IN A WOOD STOVE

EVEN IF YOU DON'T HAPPEN TO HAVE A WOOD STOVE, PERFECT CRISPY CHICKEN IS GUARANTEED WITH THIS RECIPE! MY FAVORITE SIDE DISH FOR IT IS ROSEMARY POTATO WEDGES. WHEN THE CHICKEN HAS BEEN COOKING FOR 15–20 MINUTES, ALL I DO IS PUT THE POTATOES IN THE OVEN TO COOK ALONGSIDE THE CHICKEN. BUT THE RED CABBAGE SALAD WITH FENNEL AND BLOOD ORANGE (PAGE 166) ALSO MAKES A SUPERB SIDE DISH.

1 CHICKEN, ABOUT 2.2 LB (1 KG), IDEALLY ORGANIC
1 TSP SPICE MIX (SEE BELOW)   SALT AND BLACK PEPPER
2 SPRIGS ROSEMARY   3 GARLIC CLOVES
1 PRESERVED LEMON (PAGE 25)   2 TBSP OLIVE OIL

WINTER SPICE MIX
½ TSP ALLSPICE BERRIES, 2 WHOLE CLOVES,
PINCH OF CINNAMON, ½ TSP CORIANDER SEEDS

CLASSIC SPICE MIX VARIATION
½ TSP HUNGARIAN PAPRIKA
PINCH OF CAYENNE PEPPER
PINCH OF TURMERIC
PINCH OF CUMIN

Preheat a convection oven to 400 °F (200 °C) or fire up the wood stove.

Pat the chicken dry with paper towels. To make the winter spice mix, toast the whole spices in a dry skillet, then grind together with the cinnamon using a mortar and pestle or a spice grinder. Rub the chicken inside and out with salt and pepper. Peel and thinly slice 1 garlic clove. Using your fingers, gently lift the skin away from the chicken breasts and stuff a sprig of rosemary and a few slices of garlic underneath. Cut the remaining unpeeled garlic cloves into quarters. Dice the preserved lemon. Place the garlic, lemon, and remaining rosemary into the bird's cavity.

Stir together the spice mix and the olive oil in a bowl. Using your hands or a brush, coat the chicken with the mixture and rub it lightly all over. If you like, truss the legs with kitchen twine.

Place the chicken in a roasting pan or on a baking tray breast-side down. Place it in the oven. Turn the chicken over after 30 minutes; return it to the oven. Roast for another 15 minutes, then stoke the fire or increase the heat to 435 °F (225 °C); this will make the chicken nice and crispy. If you are not pressed for time (and feel like it), you can brush the chicken with the fat that has dripped into the roasting pan.

Pierce a chicken leg with a metal skewer or knife. When the juices run clear, the chicken is done and ready to serve. If the juices are still pink, the chicken needs to cook for a few more minutes.

ROSEMARY POTATO WEDGES:

14 OZ (400 G) MINI WAXY POTATOES   1 SPRIG ROSEMARY
½ TSP COARSE SEA SALT OR FLEUR DE SEL   3 – 4 TBSP OLIVE OIL

Wash the potatoes and cut them into halves or quarters. Strip off the rosemary leaves from the stem. Place the potatoes and rosemary leaves in a small roasting pan, add the salt and oil, and toss. Bake in the oven for 40–45 minutes.

Pasta
WITH WILD GAME RAGÙ

FOR THIS WINTRY PASTA DISH, I PREFER TO USE SMALL, COMPACT PASTA SHAPES. ORECCHIETTE OR ITALIAN PASTA TYPES SUCH AS STROZZAPRETI OR MALLOREDDUS (SARDINIAN GNOCCHI) ARE A REALLY GOOD MATCH FOR THE DARK, AROMATIC RICHNESS OF THE STEW. THE GREMOLATA TOPPING ADDS A FRESH BURST OF FLAVOR.

FOR THE PASTA AND RAGÙ:
2 CARROTS   1 CELERY STALK   1 ONION
2 GARLIC CLOVES   10 OZ (300 G) WILD GAME MEAT (SUCH AS WILD BOAR OR VENISON)
SALT AND BLACK PEPPER   2 TBSP OIL, FOR FRYING   1–2 TBSP TOMATO PASTE
½ CUP (125 ML) RED WINE   2 TBSP FLOUR
1 CUP ORGANIC VEGETABLE STOCK OR WILD GAME STOCK
8 OZ (225 G) CANNED TOMATOES   4 EACH ALLSPICE BERRIES AND JUNIPER BERRIES
1 BAY LEAF   2 SPRIGS FRESH THYME, LEAVES ONLY
1 TBSP CRANBERRIES   9 OZ (250 G) SMALL DRIED PASTA, SUCH AS ORECCHIETTE

FOR THE GREMOLATA:
1 GARLIC CLOVE   1 ORGANIC LEMON, WASHED IN HOT WATER
½ BUNCH PARSLEY

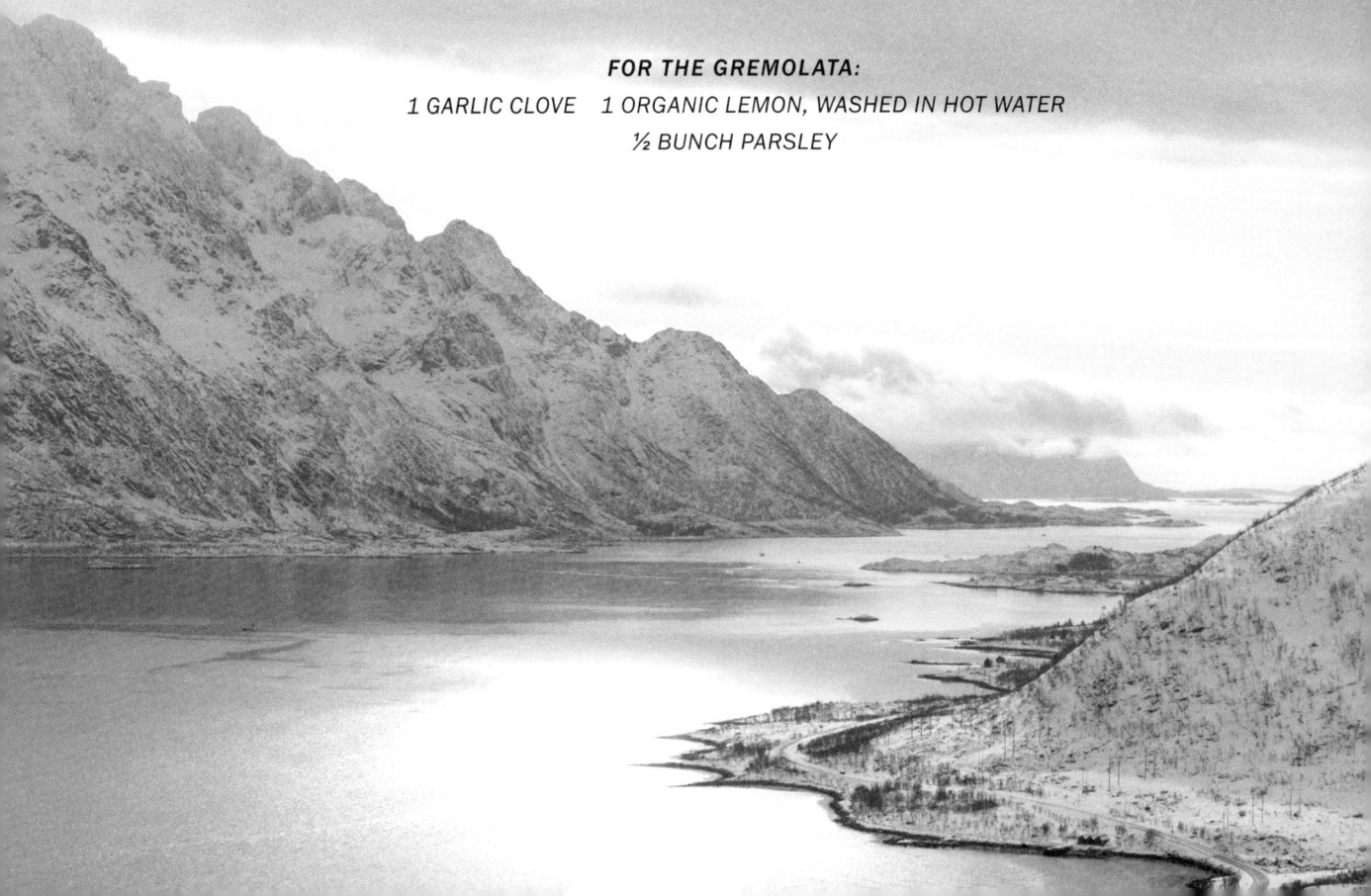

Peel and dice the carrots. Wash and dice the celery. Peel and finely chop the onion and garlic.

Cut the meat into cubes about ¾-inch (2 cm) in size. Season with salt and pepper. Heat the oil in a large pot, add the meat, and brown it on all sides. Remove meat and set aside. Add the carrots, celery, onion, and garlic to the pot, and cook in the same oil. Add the tomato paste, stir, and cook until the tomato paste starts to caramelize. Add half of the wine and deglaze by scraping up brown bits from the bottom of the pot. Cook until the liquid reduces, add the flour, and deglaze again with the remaining wine. Pour in the stock, then add the canned tomatoes.

Coarsely grind the allspice and juniper berries using a mortar and pestle. Add them to the pot along with the bay leaf. Return meat to the pot. Stir well, especially along the bottom of the pot. Cover and cook the ragù gently on the edge of the wood stove or over low heat for about 1 hour, or until the meat is very tender.

If there is too much liquid remaining, uncover the pot during the last 15 minutes of cooking time. A few minutes before the end of cooking time, add the thyme leaves and cranberries. Remove the bay leaf. Season the ragù to taste with salt and pepper.

Boil the pasta in plenty of salted water until al dente. Drain the pasta and mix it into the ragù.

To make the gremolata, peel and dice the garlic, zest the lemon, and finely chop the parsley. Mix everything together. I adore this simple mixture—it goes well with grilled fish, steak, and game, and lends a wonderful Mediterranean freshness.

★ Quick   ★ Vegetarian   ★ Energy

HEARTY PIZZOCCHERI HAILS FROM LOMBARDY. IT'S PRETTY OBVIOUS THAT THIS DISH,
WHICH FEATURES BUCKWHEAT PASTA, ORIGINATES IN THE AREA NEAR THE ITALIAN-SWISS BORDER:
THE COMBINATION OF PIZZOCCHERI NOODLES, POTATOES, AND CHEESE MAKES A HEARTY,
NOURISHING DISH, JUST PERFECT FOR COLD WEATHER. PIZZOCCHERI CAN BE SOURCED ONLINE,
AT SPECIALTY FOOD STORES, OR (IDEALLY) DURING A TRIP TO ITALY, WHERE YOU SHOULD STOCK UP WITH
A FEW PACKAGES OF PASTA. ALTERNATIVELY, YOU CAN USE WHOLEGRAIN SPELT PASTA.

Pizzoccheri

INGREDIENTS

7 OZ (200 G) POTATOES, PREFERABLY WAXY, SUCH AS YUKON GOLD
¼ SAVOY CABBAGE   SALT   5 ½ OZ (150 G) PIZZOCCHERI PASTA OR WHOLEGRAIN SPELT PASTA
1 GARLIC CLOVE   1 SPRIG SAGE   1 TBSP BUTTER
1 CUP GRATED GRUYÈRE OR PARMESAN CHEESE   BLACK PEPPER   FRESHLY GRATED NUTMEG

PREPERATION

There are several ways to cook pizzoccheri, and you can use dried or fresh pasta.
I find this one-pot version the easiest.

Peel the potatoes and cut into cubes or thin slices. Wash and slice the cabbage leaves. Fill a large pot with water
and bring to a boil. Add a generous amount of salt, then add the pasta and the potatoes. When both are still
firm to the bite, add the cabbage. Boil gently until the cabbage is tender. Drain in a colander, reserving some of the
cooking water. Peel and finely chop the garlic. Strip the sage leaves from the stem and slice them very thinly.
Melt the butter in a deep skillet, add the garlic and sage, and sauté briefly. Add the potato and pasta mixture to the
skillet and top with the grated cheese. Stir everything well, or vigorously shake the skillet back and forth.
Add some of the reserved cooking water until the consistency is nice and creamy. Season with salt, pepper, and nutmeg.
Serve straight out of the skillet.

LONG WINTER EVENINGS

EXPERT TIP

If you have a pasta maker at home, you can easily make pizzoccheri yourself. Place 5 ½ oz (150 g) buckwheat flour,
3 ½ oz (100 g) durum wheat flour, 3 large eggs and ½ teaspoon sea salt in a bowl. Knead to make a smooth
and elastic dough. Wrap the dough and let rest briefly in the refrigerator. Follow the instructions for making tagliatelle,
depending on your pasta machine, then slice into 1-inch (2 ½ cm) wide noodles. If you do use fresh noodles,
add them to the pot at the same time as the cabbage to avoid overcooking. Feel free to use other green vegetables,
such as spinach, leeks, or Swiss chard, in lieu of the cabbage.

★ Vegetarian ★ Make-ahead ★ Energy

Spinach spätzle

WITH FRIED ONIONS

THE ORIGINAL VERSION OF CHEESE SPÄTZLE COMES FROM THE ALLGÄU, AN AREA BORDERING
BAVARIA. IT IS A CLASSIC DISH SERVED IN ALPINE HUTS, ONE YOU CAN MAKE FRESH IN
NO TIME AT ALL. I HAVE CREATED AN EVEN MORE DELICIOUS VERSION. IT IS EASIEST TO MAKE
THE TINY DUMPLING-LIKE EGG NOODLES WITH A SPÄTZLE MAKER. THIS KITCHEN TOOL
HAS A LONG METAL PLATE WITH HOLES IN IT, A BIT LIKE A CHEESE GRATER, AND A HOPPER
ON TOP TO HOLD THE THICK DOUGH. YOU CAN ALSO USE A SPÄTZLE PRESS OR A POTATO
RICER. ANOTHER METHOD IS TO SPREAD THE DOUGH ON A WOODEN CUTTING BOARD AND USE
A KITCHEN SCRAPER TO CUT THIN STRIPS OF DOUGH INTO THE BOILING WATER.

203

2 SMALL ONIONS   1 TBSP FLOUR   HUNGARIAN PAPRIKA
4 TBSP SUNFLOWER OIL, FOR FRYING   2 TBSP WALNUTS
SALT   10 OZ (300 G) ALL-PURPOSE FLOUR
1 CUP FINELY CHOPPED SPINACH (OR FROZEN CREAMED SPINACH, DEFROSTED)
2–3 EGGS   FRESHLY GRATED NUTMEG   1 CUP GRATED GRUYÈRE CHEESE
1 TBSP BUTTER   BLACK PEPPER

Peel the onions and slice into thin rings. Place them in a bowl. Add 1 tablespoon of flour and a bit of paprika, and toss to combine. Heat the oil in a frying pan. Add the onions and fry until golden brown. Coarsely crush the walnuts and fry briefly with the onions. Remove the mixture from the frying pan. Drain on paper towels.

In a large pot, bring salted water to a boil. The pot should be about as wide as the spätzle maker is long. Place the flour in a bowl. Add the spinach, eggs, a bit of salt and nutmeg, and about 6 tablespoons of cold water. Mix to make a thick dough (a wooden spoon works well for this). Mix vigorously against the sides of the bowl with the spoon until the dough is elastic and bubbles form. If the dough is too dry, add a bit more water; if it is too wet, add a bit more flour. When the water boils, scoop some dough into the hopper of a spätzle maker, and place the spätzle maker over the pot. Lower heat to a simmer. Slide the hopper back and forth to push the spätzle into the barely simmering water. Repeat until all the dough is used up. Bring water back to a boil, then reduce the heat a bit and wait briefly until all the spätzle have risen to the top. Drain the spätzle in a sieve, reserving a bit of the cooking water.

Heat the butter in a frying pan until it foams. Add the spätzle and shake the pan back and forth to gently coat them with butter. Add the cheese and a bit of the reserved cooking water. Cook until the cheese is nicely melted and stringy. Season the spätzle with salt and plenty of pepper. Divide among deep plates or serve directly from the pan. Garnish with the fried onion and walnut mixture.

TIP

Spätzle can be made ahead. Drain and rinse the spätzle with cold water, toss with 1 tablespoon of oil, and refrigerate. If you would like to make classic spätzle, omit the spinach and add a bit more water to the dough instead.

LONG WINTER EVENINGS

Venison medallions

WITH CREAMED CABBAGE AND POTATO-CELERY ROOT PURÉE

SERVES 4

WINTERTIME IS WILD GAME TIME. I THINK OF WILD GAME AS ESPECIALLY SUSTAINABLE—IT IS LOCALLY SOURCED AND ALMOST ALWAYS SOLD FRESH. VENISON MEDALLIONS ARE A TRULY FESTIVE MEAL FOR SPECIAL OCCASIONS. THIS IS A DISH TO MAKE YOUR WHOLE TRIBE HAPPY, WHETHER IT'S CHRISTMAS DAY OR ANY OTHER SPECIAL DAY. DON'T BE INTIMIDATED BY ALL THE DIFFERENT DISHES. EACH ONE IS EXPLAINED STEP-BY-STEP, AND THEY ARE ALL EASY TO MAKE.

FOR THE MEDALLIONS:

1 LB 10 OZ (750 G) BONELESS LOIN OF VENISON   SALT AND BLACK PEPPER
1 TBSP FLOUR   2 TBSP OIL, FOR FRYING   ⅛ CUP (60 ML) RED WINE
½ CUP GAME STOCK OR BEEF STOCK   1 TBSP CRANBERRIES   1 TBSP COLD BUTTER

FOR THE CREAMED CABBAGE:

1 SHALLOT OR ½ ONION   1 TBSP BUTTER   ½ TBSP FLOUR
1 SMALL SAVOY CABBAGE   1 CUP (200 G) HEAVY CREAM
SALT   FRESHLY GRATED NUTMEG   ½ BUNCH PARSLEY, FINELY CHOPPED

FOR THE POTATO-CELERY ROOT PURÉE:

2.2 LB (1 KG) STARCHY POTATOES, SUCH AS RUSSET   ¼ CELERY ROOT
1 CUP MILK   SALT   FRESHLY GRATED NUTMEG   2 TBSP BUTTER

The key to a successful meal with several different dishes is being well prepared and well organized. Then everything will go smoothly and all the dishes will be served, perfectly made, at the right time.

LET'S BEGIN THE PREPARATION:
The venison should already be boneless and trimmed of all fat and silverskin. Slice it into 1-inch (2 ½ cm) thick medallions. You should end up with 8 to 12 pieces, depending on the size of the loin. Cover the medallions and set aside at room temperature; do not refrigerate.

Wash the cabbage, remove the outer leaves if needed, and cut it into quarters. Remove the core and slice the cabbage as thinly as possible. Wash and peel the potatoes. Cut larger ones in half or in quarters. Place the potatoes in cold water to prevent discoloration. Peel the celery root and cut

it into large cubes. Have all the other ingredients ready to go. Now it's time to head to the stove! Preheat the oven to 120 °F (50 °C). Warm the plates. Place the potatoes and celery root in a pot with salted water, bring to a boil, and cook until tender. This is faster (10 – 15 minutes) in a pressure cooker.

Place the cabbage in boiling salted water and blanch for 2 – 3 minutes. Remove with a slotted spoon and plunge the cabbage into an ice bath (maybe add a few cups of fresh snow into it). Transfer the cabbage to a sieve and let it drain.

Season the medallions with salt and pepper. Dredge them in the flour. Heat the oil in a stainless steel pan or cast-iron skillet. Add the medallions and sear on each side. Reduce the heat and fry for about 2 more minutes on each side.

move medallions from the skillet and put them on
e-warmed plates. Place plates in the oven to keep warm.
d the remaining flour to the skillet and cook briefly.
glaze with the red wine. Add the stock and cranberries
d cook until creamy. Season to taste with salt and
pper. Remove skillet from heat. Working very quickly,
r in the cold butter. Don't let the sauce boil any further!

make the creamed cabbage, peel and finely chop the
allot. Heat the butter in a pot. Add the shallot and sauté
til soft and translucent. Stir in the flour. Add the cabbage
d cream. Season with salt and nutmeg. Cook the
bbage briefly, stirring occasionally. Just before serving,
r in the chopped parsley.

make the potato-celery root purée, pour the milk into
ot and bring to a boil. Remove from heat and season the
milk with salt and nutmeg. Drain the cooked potatoes
and celery root. Either press the potatoes and celery
root into the milk through a potato press, or place
them in a separate pot, mash with a potato masher,
and pour the milk over. Cut the butter into small pieces
and add it to the potato mixture. Whisk gently. For
a fluffy texture, do not overwork the whisk or the purée
will turn gluey.

To serve, divide the potato-celery root purée and
the cabbage among warm plates, arrange the venison
medallions on the plates, and top with a bit of the
cranberry sauce.

To elevate the dish even further, accompany with half
a pear poached in white wine and sugar and topped with
cranberries. Merry Christmas and a happy holiday season!

IF YOU'VE BEEN TO THE ALPS, CHANCES ARE YOU HAVE SAMPLED POTATO NOODLES (OR "FINGER DUMPLINGS") IN ONE OF THE HUTS, WHERE THEY ARE KNOWN AS *SCHUPFNUDELN*. THOSE NOODLES ARE USUALLY PACKAGED, BUT YOU CAN JUST AS EASILY MAKE THE LITTLE DELICACIES YOURSELF. AND THE TASTE WILL BE WORLDS APART.

Potato noodles
WITH SAUERKRAUT

SERVES 2

FOR THE POTATO NOODLES:
9 OZ (250 G) STARCHY POTATOES, SUCH AS RUSSET   SALT
1 EGG YOLK   3–4 TBSP ALL-PURPOSE FLOUR   FRESHLY GRATED NUTMEG

1 JAR (12 OZ / 350 G) SAUERKRAUT   1 BAY LEAF   1 SMALL ONION
1 TBSP BUTTER OR LARD   SALT AND BLACK PEPPER   1 BUNCH CHIVES

OPTIONAL:
3 ½ OZ (100 G) DICED SMOKED BACON

Boil the potatoes in a pot of salted water for 20 minutes, or until tender. When cool enough to handle, peel and press the potatoes through a ricer into a bowl, or mash with a potato masher. Let the steam evaporate completely. Add the egg yolk and flour, and combine. Season to taste with salt and nutmeg. Knead to make a smooth dough.

Place the dough on a lightly floured work surface. Shape the dough into a long, thin roll about ½-inch (1 ¼ cm) wide. Cut the dough into 2-inch (5 cm) pieces. Roll each piece between your palms to form dumpling-shaped thick noodles with pointed ends.

Bring a pot of salted water to a boil. Add the noodles, reduce the heat, and simmer until the noodles float to the surface. Remove them with a slotted spoon. Drain briefly and fry immediately, or shock the noodles in plenty of cold water and then drain them. Refrigerate until ready to use.

Place the sauerkraut and the bay leaf in a pot, cover, and heat slowly. Peel and finely dice the onion. Heat the butter or lard in a large frying pan, add the onion, and sauté. If using bacon, add it to the pan and cook with the onion. Add the noodles and fry on all sides until golden brown. Drain the sauerkraut well and add it to the noodles. Mix everything together well. Season to taste with salt and pepper. Garnish with plenty of chopped chives and serve straight from the pan, family-style, or divide the noodles among deep plates.

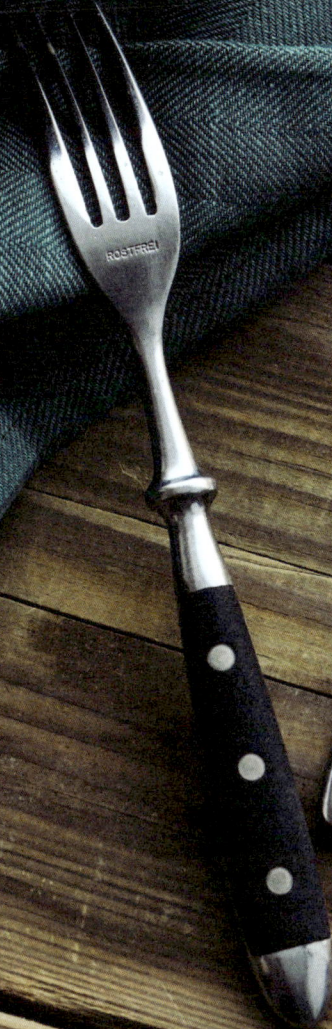

CHEESE DUMPLINGS ARE ANOTHER HEARTY CULINARY DELIGHT
FROM TYROL, AND A TRUE ALPINE HUT CLASSIC. WHETHER YOU SERVE THEM
VERY TRADITIONALLY IN CLEAR BEEF STOCK (PAGE 188) OR AS
A QUICK LUNCH WITH A CRISP WINTER SALAD, THEY ARE ALWAYS A HIT!
TRY THEM ALSO AS A SIDE DISH FOR MEAT, OR REIMAGINE THEM AS A VEGGIE
BURGER OF SORTS WITH A SIDE OF POTATO SALAD.

Bread dumplings
WITH ALPINE CHEESE

SERVES 2

10 OZ (300 G) DAY-OLD BREAD OR BUNS
7 OZ (200 G) CRUMBLED TYROLEAN GRAY CHEESE
OR GRATED GRUYÈRE   1 ONION
3 TBSP BUTTER   ¾ CUP (200 ML) MILK
SALT AND BLACK PEPPER   3 – 4 EGGS
½ BUNCH PARSLEY AND/OR CHIVES, CHOPPED
1 TBSP VEGETABLE OIL, FOR FRYING

Cut the bread or buns into small pieces and
place them in a bowl. Add the cheese and mix to
combine. Peel and finely chop the onion. Heat
1 tablespoon of the butter in a small sauté pan. Add the
onion and sauté until soft and translucent.
Warm the milk. Add the milk and onions to the bread
mixture, and season with salt and pepper.
Add the eggs and chopped herbs and combine well.
Let the mixture stand for 15 minutes. Moisten your hands
and shape the mixture into medium-sized dumplings.
Flatten the dumplings slightly between your hands. Heat
the remaining 2 tablespoons of butter and the
oil in a frying pan. Fry the dumplings over medium heat
on both sides until golden yellow.

★ *Vegetarian* ★ *Energy*

THESE DELICIOUS POTATO DOUGHNUTS ARE A MARVELOUS, CRISPY FIRST COURSE—
A KIND OF ALPINE TAPAS, IF YOU WILL. THEY ARE RELATIVELY QUICK TO PREPARE, AND
YOU CAN CUSTOMIZE THE FILLINGS TO YOUR HEART'S DESIRE. FOR STARTERS, YOU CAN
ADD A FEW PIECES OF DICED BACON TO THE POTATO MIXTURE NEXT TIME!

ZILLER VALLEY
Potato doughnuts

SERVES 2

FOR THE FILLING:
4 (ABOUT 1 LB 2 OZ / 500 G)
STARCHY POTATOES,
SUCH AS RUSSET
1 CUP (250 G) FRESH CHEESE,
SUCH AS QUARK, RICOTTA,
OR SOUR CREAM
1 EGG YOLK
1 TSP CORNSTARCH
SALT AND BLACK PEPPER
FRESHLY GRATED NUTMEG
1 BUNCH CHIVES, CHOPPED

FOR THE DOUGH:
10 OZ (300 G) RYE OR SPELT FLOUR
5 ½ OZ (150 G) ALL-PURPOSE
FLOUR
½ CUP MILK
½ TSP SALT
FAT OR VEGETABLE OIL, FOR FRYING

FOR THE DIP:
½ RIPE AVOCADO
½ CUP SOUR CREAM
JUICE OF ½ LEMON
SALT AND BLACK PEPPER
SRIRACHA SAUCE

To make the filling, boil the potatoes in a pot of salted water for about 20 minutes, or until tender. Drain and peel the potatoes; set aside until the steam evaporates. In a bowl, mash the potatoes. Add the cheese, egg yolk, and cornstarch, and combine well. Mix in the salt, pepper, nutmeg, and chives.

To make the dough, mix together the flours and salt. Add the milk bit by bit, kneading after each addition. Knead vigorously until the dough is firm. Let rest briefly. Cut the dough in half. Shape each half into a log as thick as a zucchini. Moisten a knife with water and cut each log into about 20 slices. Transfer the slices onto a lightly floured work surface. Using your hands or a rolling pin, flatten each piece into a disk.

To fill the doughnuts, moisten 2 teaspoons and scoop out portions of the potato filling. Place the filling in the center of each piece of dough. Fold the dough over and press the edges together firmly to seal. Heat the fat or oil in a large pot or deep fryer. Add the doughnuts in batches and fry until golden brown. Remove with a slotted spoon and drain on paper towels.

To make the dip, peel the avocado. Place it in a small bowl and mash with a fork. Stir in the sour cream and lemon juice. Season with salt, pepper, and sriracha sauce.

TIP

A crunchy winter salad with mâche, Belgian endive, and walnuts accompanies the doughnuts perfectly.

HERE IS A RECIPE FOR ORIGINAL SWABIAN RAVIOLI FROM SCRATCH, COURTESY
OF OUR FRIEND HEIDI. HEIDI IS, OF COURSE, FROM SWABIA. THIS DISH, CALLED *MAULTASCHEN*
IN GERMAN, BRINGS BACK MEMORIES OF OUR BACKCOUNTRY SKIING TRIPS TOGETHER
IN NORTHERN NORWAY. WE ALWAYS RELISHED EATING THE HOMEMADE RAVIOLI HEIDI BROUGHT
ALONG ON THESE TRIPS. THEY WERE A TASTE OF HOME AND A SOURCE OF HEARTY
SUSTENANCE AFTER AN ESPECIALLY TIRING DAY OF BACKCOUNTRY SKIING.

Swabian ravioli

SERVES 4–6

FOR THE DOUGH:
14 OZ (400 G) PASTRY FLOUR
½ CUP WATER
1 TBSP WHITE VINEGAR
4 TBSP SUNFLOWER OIL
½ TSP SALT

FOR THE FILLING:
1 SMALL ONION
3 ½ OZ (100 G) SMOKED HAM SAUSAGE
3 ½ OZ (100 G) SPINACH (OPTIONAL)
1 BUNCH PARSLEY
1–2 DAY-OLD BREAD ROLLS
14 OZ (400 G) MIXED GROUND PORK AND BEEF
7 OZ (200 G) SAUSAGE MEAT
1–2 EGGS, DEPENDING ON THE SIZE
2 ½ OZ (75 G) ALL-PURPOSE FLOUR
SALT, BLACK PEPPER, FRESHLY GRATED NUTMEG,
GARLIC POWDER

BEEF STOCK (PAGE 188), FOR BOILING (OR WATER)

To make the dough, place all dough ingredients in a bowl and knead until smooth, elastic, and shiny. Let rest for about 15 minutes. (Alternatively, you can buy fresh lasagna sheets to use instead of the dough.)

To make the filling, peel and finely dice the onion. Using a food processor or a knife, finely chop the ham sausage. If using spinach, blanch, drain, and chop it finely. Wash and finely chop the parsley. Cut the bread rolls into large cubes. Soften them in a small bowl of warm water, then squeeze out the water. Place the onion, ham sausage, spinach, if using, and bread in a bowl. Stir in the remaining ingredients and combine thoroughly with your hands. Season generously with salt, black pepper, nutmeg, and garlic powder.

Roll out the dough on a floured work surface to a ¹⁄₁₆–⅛-in (2–3 mm) thickness. A pasta maker, if you have one, makes light work of this step. Cut the dough into 6-inch (15 cm) squares. Place 1–2 tablespoons of the filling on each square. Fold to make a rectangle. Using a fork, press down firmly on the edges to seal.

In a pot, bring beef stock or salted water to a boil. Gently slide the ravioli into the water, decrease the heat, and simmer for about 10 minutes. Using a slotted spoon, remove the ravioli from the water and plunge them into an ice bath. Add a few drops of oil to prevent them from sticking together.

This recipe makes about 4–6 servings. Leftover ravioli freeze extremely well. You can also vacuum-seal the ravioli and refrigerate for up to about 2 weeks.

Swabian ravioli
BAKED IN CREAM

2 LEEKS   3 ½ OZ (100 G) COOKED HAM   ½ CUP HEAVY CREAM   ½ CUP CRÈME FRAÎCHE
SALT AND BLACK PEPPE   1 TBSP BUTTER, FOR GREASING   HANDFUL OF SHAVED PARMESAN

Preheat the oven to 360 °F (180 °C). Wash and very thinly slice the leeks. Cut the ham into strips. Place the heavy cream and crème fraîche in a bowl. Add the leeks and ham, and stir to combine. Season to taste with salt and pepper. Butter a heatproof casserole dish and arrange 6–8 ravioli on the bottom. Pour the cream mixture over the ravioli, and scatter Parmesan shavings on top. Bake for about 35 minutes, or until the ravioli are golden brown. This dish tastes fabulous served with a crunchy winter salad!

Of course, you can always go traditional and serve the ravioli in a soup. Or, cut them into strips, fry them in a bit of butter, and there you have it: a mouthwatering hash.

Bread dumplings

BASIC BREAD DUMPLINGS

1 ONION   ½ BUNCH PARSLEY
1 TBSP BUTTER
1 CUP HOT MILK   SALT
BLACK PEPPER
FRESHLY GRATED NUTMEG
9 OZ (250 G) DAY-OLD WHITE BREAD, BUNS,
OR BAGUETTE, CUT INTO CUBES
2–3 EGGS

Peel and dice the onion. Wash and finely chop the parsley. Melt the butter in a frying pan. Add the onion and sauté until soft and translucent. Season the milk with salt, pepper, and nutmeg. Place the bread in a bowl and pour the hot milk over it. Add the onion and parsley to the bowl. Beat the eggs, add them to the bread mixture, and mix to combine. If the mixture is too wet, add 1–2 tablespoons of breadcrumbs. If it is too dry, add a bit more milk.

Bring plenty of water to a boil in a large pot. Add ½ teaspoon of salt. Moisten your hands with water and shape the bread mixture into small, round dumplings. Carefully place the dumplings into the boiling water. Boil over medium heat for 5 minutes, then reduce the heat. Simmer until the dumplings are cooked, about 10 minutes. When the dumplings float to the top and roll over, they are ready.

SPINACH AND CHEESE DUMPLINGS

2–3 HANDFULS FRESH SPINACH
(OR 2 CUBES FROZEN SPINACH, DEFROSTED)
1 SMALL GARLIC CLOVE, CHOPPED
5 ½ OZ (150 G) GRUYÈRE CHEESE (OR MEDIUM GOUDA CHEESE)

Follow the basic recipe, but add the spinach and garlic to the frying pan with the onion and sauté briefly. Cut the cheese into cubes and fold it in when you are mixing the bread with the other ingredients.

BACON DUMPLINGS

Finely dice 3 ½ oz (100 g) of bacon. Add it to the frying pan with the onion, fry until crisp, then proceed as in the basic recipe.

RED BEET DUMPLINGS

Finely chop or grate 1 cooked, peeled red beet (cooked and peeled beets are also available in vacuum packs). Ideally, use rubber gloves when handling the beet, or it will stain your hands. Fold in the beet when you are mixing the bread with the other ingredients, and proceed as in the basic recipe.

TIP

Pick your three favorite kinds of dumplings, then mix and match them into a single dish. Fry 4 tablespoons of breadcrumbs in butter until golden brown. Scatter the breadcrumbs over the mixed dumplings. A few arugula leaves and shavings of Parmesan cheese on top round out the flavors, and there you go: a very tasty meal.

Cooked dumplings freeze well. Leftover dumplings are delicious when cut into slices and fried, as in the South Tyrolean Dumpling Salad on page 161.

Pretzel casserole

WITH WALNUTS

ARE YOU IN THE MOOD FOR SOMETHING OTHER THAN THE USUAL BREAD DUMPLINGS
TO PAIR WITH YOUR HEARTY ROAST? DO YOU HAVE SOFT PRETZELS LEFT OVER FROM THE DAY BEFORE?
IF SO, TRY THIS CRUNCHY CASSEROLE, WHICH IS A GOOD COMPANION FOR OTHER ROBUST
MEAT DISHES AS WELL, LIKE THE HEARTY GOULASH (PAGE 187).

6 – 8 SOFT DAY-OLD PRETZELS
1 ONION   2 TBSP BUTTER   1 CUP (250 ML) MILK
SALT, BLACK PEPPER, FRESHLY GRATED NUTMEG
2 – 3 EGGS, BEATEN   ½ BUNCH PARSLEY, FINELY CHOPPED
3 – 4 TBSP COARSELY CRUSHED WALNUTS
HANDFUL OF GRATED GRUYÈRE CHEESE

Rub some of the salt off the pretzels. Cut pretzels into ½-inch (1 ¼ cm) slices. Place the pieces
in a large bowl. Peel and dice the onion. Heat 1 ½ tablespoons of the butter in a skillet.
Add the onions and sauté until soft and translucent. Add the milk to the skillet and cook until just
warm. Season to taste with salt, pepper, and nutmeg. Pour the mixture over the pretzel pieces.
Add the eggs, parsley, and walnuts. Combine well, and let stand for about 15 minutes.

Preheat the oven to 360 °F (180 °C). Grease a heatproof casserole dish with the remaining
butter. Transfer the pretzel mixture to the dish. Sprinkle with the grated cheese. Bake for
25 – 30 minutes on the middle rack of the oven, until the casserole is a lovely golden brown.
Use a large cookie cutter or a cup to portion out servings, or use a knife to cut out
diamond-shaped portions. Keep warm until serving time.

TIP

Use leftover pretzel casserole in Tyrolean Hash (page 194) instead of potatoes,
or fry leftover slices to make a tasty snack.

LONG WINTER EVENINGS

WINTRY DESSERTS

WINTRY DESSERTS

FLOUR-BASED DESSERTS ARE KNOWN AS *MEHLSPEISEN* IN GERMAN.
THE SOUND OF THIS WORD ALONE IS ENOUGH TO MAKE
THE MOUTHS OF KNOWING GERMAN-SPEAKERS WATER. MOST OF THESE
DESSERTS WERE TRADITIONALLY AUSTRIAN, BUT MORE RECENT
INCARNATIONS FOUND ELSEWHERE ARE ALSO TANTALIZINGLY DELICIOUS.
THIS TYPE OF DESSERT CAN BE SERVED AT THE END OF A LONG, LEISURELY DINNER,
BUT WHAT MAKES IT SPECIAL IS THAT IT CAN DOUBLE AS A SWEET MAIN COURSE
OR A SNACK. *MEHLSPEISEN* ARE SINFULLY GOOD, AND ARE ALWAYS A HIT.

A BRIEF GUIDE TO AVALANCHES
PAGE 230 – 233

THESE SMALL DUMPLINGS MADE WITH FRESH CHEESE ARE A CULINARY DELIGHT
AND A FESTIVE DESSERT. MAYBE YOU ARE FAMILIAR WITH THEM FROM TRADITIONAL AUSTRIAN CUISINE.
THE RECIPE WELCOMES VARIATIONS; FOR EXAMPLE, TRY FILLING THE DUMPLINGS WITH HALF
OF A PLUM OR APRICOT.

Fresh-cheese dumplings

SERVES 2

1 OZ (25 G) BUTTER   ¾ OZ (20 G) POWDERED SUGAR
ZEST OF 1 ORGANIC LEMON OR ORGANIC ORANGE (OR A MIX OF BOTH)
SEEDS OF ½ VANILLA BEAN
1 CUP (250 G) FRESH CHEESE, SUCH AS QUARK, RICOTTA, OR SOUR CREAM
3 ½ OZ (100 G) BREADCRUMBS (OR EQUAL PARTS SEMOLINA FLOUR AND BREADCRUMBS)
1 EGG   1 EGG YOLK   1 TBSP SUGAR AND 1 TSP SALT, FOR THE COOKING WATER

FOR THE BREADCRUMB TOPPING:
1 CUP BREADCRUMBS   3 TBSP BUTTER
4 HEAPING TBSP SUGAR   PINCH OF CINNAMON

All the ingredients should be at room temperature.
This is especially important for the butter, eggs, and cheese.

In a bowl, beat the butter and powdered sugar together until light and fluffy. Stir in the
lemon zest and vanilla seeds. Add the cheese, then the breadcrumbs, egg, and egg
yolk. Stir the mixture until smooth. Cover and let rest for at least 1 hour in the
refrigerator (or, if you are in the mountains, in front of the hut).

Fill a large pot with water and bring to a gentle boil. Add the sugar and salt.
Moisten your hands with water and shape the mixture into small, round dumplings.
Place them carefully in the boiling water. Reduce the heat to a simmer and cook the
dumplings. Meanwhile, make the topping. Heat the butter in a frying pan.
Add the breadcrumbs and fry until golden brown. Turn the breadcrumbs out onto a
large plate, sprinkle with the sugar and cinnamon, and mix to combine.
When the dumplings rise to the top of the water and roll over, they are done.
Remove from the water with a slotted spoon and coat with breadcrumb mixture.

These dumplings are delicious served with Caramelized Plum Compote (there is a
recipe for it in *The Great Outdoors* summer book, page 31). Or, just adding a scoop of
vanilla ice cream will take them to the next level of deliciousness.

223

WINTRY DESSERTS

Fluffy yeast dumplings

SERVES 4

WHEN I WAS A KID, MY GRANDMOTHER'S HOUSE WAS OFTEN FILLED
WITH THE SEDUCTIVE AROMA OF OVEN-FRESH, FLUFFY YEAST DUMPLINGS.
TRADITIONALLY, THEY ARE BAKED WITHOUT A FILLING;
SOMETIMES RAISINS ARE ADDED TO THE DOUGH. THERE IS ALSO
A PLUM-FILLED VERSION. TO ME, THEY TASTE BEST WITH THE COLD VANILLA
SAUCE FROM MY FRENCH TOAST RECIPE (PAGE 238), OR WITH CARAMELIZED
PLUM COMPOTE (*THE GREAT OUTDOORS* SUMMER BOOK, PAGE 31).

1 LB 2 OZ (500 G) ALL-PURPOSE FLOUR OR BREAD FLOUR
2 TSP ACTIVE DRY YEAST
3 ½ OZ (100 G) CANE SUGAR
⅔ CUP (150 ML) MILK
1 ¾ OZ (50 G) BUTTER
3 EGGS
ZEST OF ½ ORGANIC LEMON

Sift the flour into a large bowl. Stir in the yeast and
half of the sugar. Place the milk in a small saucepan. Warm the
milk over low heat, then add the butter. When the butter has
melted, stir the warm milk (it must not be too hot!) into the flour.
Add 2 of the eggs and the lemon zest. Knead everything together to make
a smooth and elastic dough. Cover the dough with a kitchen towel and let
it rise in a warm place until it has doubled in volume, about 30 minutes.

In the meantime, grease a roasting pan or baking dish with butter.
Preheat the oven to 360 °F (180 °C).

When the dough has risen, knead it well then shape it into 8–10 balls. Place the
dough balls on a floured tray or baking sheet and let rise again for 20 minutes.

Separate the remaining egg. Beat the yolk in a small bowl.
Place the dumplings in the prepared pan or baking dish. Brush the egg yolk
over the dumplings. Bake on the middle oven rack for 30 minutes or until
golden brown. Serve immediately.

Pack up the leftovers and take them to the mountains!

WINTRY DESSERTS

Apple strudel

WITH
CARAMELIZED WALNUTS

STRUDELS ARE A STAPLE OF AUSTRIAN CUISINE.
THEY CAN BE MADE WITH EITHER SWEET OR SAVORY FILLINGS.
APPLE STRUDEL, ALONGSIDE FRESH CHEESE STRUDEL,
BELONGS TO THE PANTHEON OF PAPER-THIN DOUGH CLASSICS.
YOU CAN READILY BUY FROZEN STRUDEL DOUGH,
BUT DO TRY MAKING IT YOURSELF; THE ONLY WAY TO GET THE
REAL STRUDEL TASTE IS BY KNEADING AND STRETCHING THE
DOUGH OUT WITH YOUR OWN TWO HANDS!

SERVES 8

FOR THE STRUDEL DOUGH:
2 TBSP SUNFLOWER OIL   PINCH OF SALT
½ TSP LEMON JUICE (OPTIONAL)
7 OZ (200 G) ALL-PURPOSE FLOUR

FOR THE CARAMELIZED WALNUTS:
3 OZ (80 G) DARK CANE SUGAR
2 TBSP WATER   3 OZ (80 G) WALNUTS

FOR THE FILLING:
2.2 LB (1 KG) SLIGHTLY SOUR APPLES, IDEALLY HOMEGROWN
JUICE OF ½ LEMON   4 TBSP RAISINS
3 TBSP RUM OR WATER   1 ½ OZ (40 G) BUTTER
2 TBSP BREADCRUMBS   1 TSP CINNAMON
1 ¾ OZ (50 G) CANE SUGAR

FOR THE TOPPING:
1 EGG YOLK   2 TBSP HEAVY CREAM
POWDERED SUGAR

To make the dough, combine the oil, salt and lemon juice, if using, in a large mixing bowl. Add ½ cup (120 ml) warm water and about half of the flour. Stir vigorously with a wooden spoon. Add the remaining flour. Using the spoon at first and then your hands, incorporate it into the dough. As soon as the dough is smooth and elastic, turn it out onto the work surface. Knead vigorously for 10 minutes. The dough should be moist but not sticky. If it is too sticky, dust with a bit more flour and knead to incorporate. Let the dough rest for 1 hour at room temperature.

To make the caramelized walnuts, add the sugar and 2 tablespoons water to a skillet and heat until lightly caramelized. Add the walnuts and stir to coat with caramel. Place the walnuts on parchment paper to cool, then coarsely chop them.

Preheat the oven to 375 °F (190 °C). Line a baking tray with parchment paper.

To make the filling, peel and quarter the apples. Core each quarter, then cut it into small pieces. Place cut apples in a large bowl. Stir in the lemon juice. Soak the raisins in rum (or in warm water for an alcohol-free version). Melt the butter in a frying pan. Add the breadcrumbs and fry until golden brown. Add the buttery breadcrumbs, cinnamon, sugar, and soaked raisins to the apples. Stir to combine.

Flour a clean cloth. Roll the dough out onto the cloth very thinly to form a long rectangle. Using your hands, carefully stretch out the dough on all sides. Place the filling lengthwise along the lower third of the dough. Scatter the caramelized walnuts over the filling, leaving a border from the edges. Using the cloth, fold the dough in from the sides, then roll it up carefully. Place the strudel on the baking tray seam-side down.

In a small bowl, beat together the egg yolk and cream. Place the strudel in the oven and bake for 20 minutes. After 20 minutes, remove from the oven and brush with the egg wash. Return strudel to the oven and bake for another 10 minutes or until golden brown. Remove and dust with powdered sugar. Let the strudel cool slightly, cut it into pieces, and serve warm.

The strudel is heavenly with whipped cream and/or a scoop of ice cream, or with the vanilla sauce on page 238.

I'D KEPT THIS BEAUTIFUL, FESTIVE DESSERT A SECRET
FOR A LONG TIME. I PREPARED IT OFTEN WHEN I WORKED AS A PASTRY
CHEF IN TOP KITCHENS. IT TASTES BEST HOT, WITH A SCOOP
OF VANILLA OR WALNUT ICE CREAM ON THE SIDE.

★ *Deluxe* ★ *Wood stove*

Fresh-cheese crepes

BAKED IN CUSTARD

SERVES 2-3

FOR THE CREPES:
4 ½ OZ (125 G) ALL-PURPOSE FLOUR   ½ CUP (125 ML) MILK
1–2 EGGS   PINCH OF SALT   1 TBSP SUNFLOWER OIL, FOR FRYING

Place the flour in a bowl. Add a bit of milk and stir until smooth. Stir in the remaining milk, eggs, and salt.
Grease a medium non-stick skillet with oil. Cook the crepes one at a time until golden brown on both sides.

FOR THE FILLING:
2 TBSP (30 G) BUTTER   1 CUP (250 G) FRESH CHEESE, SUCH AS QUARK, RICOTTA, OR SOUR CREAM
3 OZ (90 G) BROWN SUGAR   1 EGG   1 TBSP RUM
ZEST OF ½ ORGANIC ORANGE   2 TBSP VANILLA PUDDING POWDER

Melt the butter. Place it in a bowl or a food processor. Add all other ingredients and either whisk
by hand or mix in the food processor. Briefly place the mixture in the refrigerator.

FOR THE CUSTARD:
1 CUP (250 ML) MILK   1 ¾ OZ (50 G) (BROWN) SUGAR
3 EGGS   SEEDS OF ½ VANILLA BEAN

Whisk together all the ingredients. Strain the custard through a very fine-mesh sieve.

Preheat the oven to 300 °F (150 °C). Grease a shallow baking dish with butter. Lay out the crepes and
spread some of the filling evenly over each one. Roll up the crepes and pack them tightly into the baking dish.
Pour the custard over the crepes. Bake for 20–30 minutes. Let cool a bit, then cut into diamond-shaped pieces.
Arrange on plates, dust with powdered sugar, and serve with ice cream.

THESE THIN CREPES FILLED WITH FRUITY GOODNESS ARE AN IDEAL
DESSERT. THEY ARE QUICK TO PREPARE, AND A FUN KITCHEN PROJECT FOR
KIDS TO HELP WITH. IN FALL, WHEN YOU COME ACROSS FRESH
CRANBERRIES AT THE MARKET, DON'T THINK TWICE: GRAB SOME, GO HOME,
AND MAKE CRANBERRY JAM.

★ *Quick* ★ *Energy*

Crepes

FILLED WITH CRANBERRY JAM

SERVES 4

FOR THE CREPES:
14 OZ (400 G) ALL-PURPOSE FLOUR
1 ¾ CUPS (400 ML) MILK
1 TBSP BROWN SUGAR
PINCH OF SALT
3 – 4 EGGS
SUNFLOWER OIL, FOR FRYING
4 TBSP CRANBERRY JAM
1 TBSP POWDERED SUGAR, FOR DUSTING

Place the flour in a bowl. Add a bit of the milk and stir until the mixture is smooth and lump-free.
Stir in the remaining milk, sugar, salt, and eggs. Grease a non-stick skillet with the oil.
Spreading the batter as thinly as possible, cook the crepes until golden brown on both sides.
Spread the cranberry jam over the crepes, then either roll them up or fold them in half.
Dust with powdered sugar and serve immediately.
A scoop of vanilla ice cream always makes everything better.

TIP

You can never go wrong with the chocolate version, either.
Replace the cranberry jam with chocolate spread,
place a few thin slices of banana on top, roll up or fold, and enjoy.

WINTRY DESSERTS

A brief guide to avalanches

Great weather is a prerequisite for a perfect time on skis or a snowboard. And so is snow, snow, and more snow. But snow also has its risks. To help you stay safe when you are in the mountains, I have compiled a brief guide to avalanches for you. Of course, this is just an overview of key points. This is why I highly recommend you prepare by taking an avalanche training course each season, before heading out to spend time in the snow.

Whether you are on a backcountry skiing tour or freeriding, you will never be able to completely eliminate risk. Careful, deliberate action is the only way to ensure that you enjoy your sport for as long as possible. Some basic information follows.

MANY FACTORS PLAY A LARGE ROLE IN AVALANCHE FORMATION:

> ✗ Weather—A large amount of fresh snow coupled with wind and cold temperatures increases the danger of an avalanche.
> ✗ Terrain—On unmarked and steep slopes (30° or steeper) there is a high probability of avalanches.
> ✗ Snowpack—A slab avalanche is released when there is a weak layer under the surface of the existing snowpack.
> ✗ Human factor—Even when the temptation of a slope is very strong, act responsibly and behave defensively to lower the risk and better recognize the danger signs.

The most important factor in detecting avalanche risk and avoiding avalanches is the human factor. Experience, know-how, individual skill, and behaving according to the conditions are key factors for a safe mountain tour. For any backcountry tour or on-piste activity, it is essential to plan meticulously, observe your surroundings closely, and, when making decisions, always keep risk in mind.

AVALANCHE EMERGENCY EQUIPMENT

In case of emergency, having a *complete set of avalanche emergency equipment* on hand enables your friends to locate you and dig you out. Whenever you leave marked ski areas, you must *always* carry *standard personal emergency equipment* with you. **PLEASE NOTE:** you will only have a chance of digging your friends out alive from under an avalanche if you have a complete set of emergency equipment with you. Keep in mind that emergency equipment won't prevent you from being swept up or buried under an avalanche yourself!

ESSENTIAL EMERGENCY EQUIPMENT:

> ✗ Beacons/transceivers—3 receiving antennas and a marking function are standard.
> ✗ Shovel—A snow shovel with a serrated blade can save you vital time.
> ✗ Probe—A sturdy avalanche probe that is quickly assembled is essential.

BEFORE LEAVING—AVALANCHE FORECAST

Getting ready for a backcountry skiing tour involves not only having the proper equipment, but also checking the avalanche forecast. This is usually updated daily throughout the ski season. An avalanche forecast compiles information from automated stations, observers, snow profiles, and people with knowledge of the area. Since a brief look at the avalanche hazard level does not provide enough information, check the local avalanche reports for information on the weather, snow cover, avalanche hazard level (the dangerous areas, the extra weight the snow can bear, the chance of triggering an avalanche), and for a forecast of how conditions will develop. The local avalanche forecast can be found either online or in the backcountry area itself, at the lowest lift station.

STARTING OUT—BEACON CHECK

Since every activity is more fun with friends, always find a partner for your backcountry travels. In an emergency, your partner can be your lifeline. To help you start off your backcountry tour right, here are a few steps for a successful partner beacon check.

At your starting point, check **ALL THE BEACONS/ TRANSCEIVERS** to make sure they are transmitting and receiving properly.

GROUP LEADER CHECK:

✗ The leader sets his/her beacon to send (transmit) mode;
✗ All the other group members set their beacons to search (receive) mode.

GROUP MEMBER CHECK:

✗ The leader sets his/her beacon to search (receive) mode, all the others to send (transmit);
✗ One by one, at a distance of 16–33 ft (5–10 m) from each other, the group members walk past the leader;
✗ When the check is successful, the leader also sets his/her device to send mode.

Double-check the battery strength in all the beacon/transceivers before every backcountry tour. Replace any weak batteries with fresh ones. If a battery has less than a 50% charge, it must be replaced with a fully charged one. Carrying spare batteries with you is always a good idea.

Apple fritters
IN WHEAT BEER BATTER

APPLE FRITTERS TASTE BEST SERVED WITH A SCOOP OF ICE CREAM (OF COURSE).
THE BATTER CAN BE PREPARED QUICKLY, AND THE BASIC RECIPE ALLOWS FOR A GREAT
DEAL OF EXPERIMENTATION. SAVORY INGREDIENTS, SUCH AS VEGETABLES OR FISH
FILLETS, ALSO TASTE DELICIOUS FRIED IN THIS BATTER. IF YOU USE SAVORY INGREDIENTS,
YOU CAN ALSO ADD SPICES, LIKE CURRY, TO TWEAK THE BATTER.

FOR THE BEER BATTER:
9 OZ (250 G) ALL-PURPOSE FLOUR
(1 CUP / 250 ML) WHEAT BEER
(IF THERE IS BEER LEFT OVER, DRINK IT WELL CHILLED)
1 EGG YOLK
2 TBSP SUNFLOWER OIL
2 EGG WHITES
PINCH OF SALT

To make the batter, mix the flour, beer, egg yolk, and oil until smooth. Beat the egg whites and salt together
in a separate bowl until soft peaks form. Using a whisk, carefully fold the egg whites into the batter.

FOR THE FRITTERS:
2 APPLES
OIL (SUCH AS PEANUT OIL) OR LARD, FOR FRYING
4 TBSP CINNAMON SUGAR
POWDERED SUGAR (OPTIONAL)

To make the fritters, peel the apples and core them using an apple corer. Cut the apples into ½-inch (1 ¼ cm)
thick rounds. In a shallow saucepan or frying pan, heat 2 inches (5 cm) of oil or lard (be careful if
children are around!). Dip each apple round in batter, draining off the excess, and immediately fry in the
hot oil until golden brown on both sides. Drain on paper towels. Dip the fritters in the cinnamon sugar, then
dust with powdered sugar, if desired. Serve immediately with a scoop of vanilla ice cream, if available.

VARIATION
Do try using sliced pears or halved apricots instead of apples at some point!

WINTRY DESSERTS

FRENCH TOAST IS ALWAYS A PERFECT WAY TO USE UP
DAY-OLD WHITE BREAD AND TURN IT INTO A TASTY DESSERT. I ALSO LOVE
FRENCH TOAST SERVED WITH A SLIGHTLY SOUR CHERRY COMPOTE.

★ *Quick* ★ *Energy*

French toast
WITH VANILLA SAUCE

SERVES 2

FOR THE VANILLA SAUCE:
1 VANILLA BEAN
2 CUPS (500 ML) MILK
2 OZ (60 G) SUGAR
4 EGG YOLKS
½ TSP CORNSTARCH (OPTIONAL)

To make the vanilla sauce, split the vanilla bean lengthwise and scrape out the seeds. In a saucepan, heat the vanilla seeds, vanilla bean, milk, and half of the sugar, and boil briefly. In a bowl, whisk the egg yolks with the remaining sugar until foamy. Whisking constantly, add the hot milk a bit at a time. Place the bowl over a double boiler. Whisking vigorously, cook until the sauce has reached the "rose stage." (Dip a wooden spoon into the sauce and gently blow on the back of the spoon. If circular rose-like petals form, it is ready.) If you would like a thicker sauce, whisk in ½ teaspoon cornstarch as you are heating the milk.

FOR THE FRENCH TOAST:
¾ CUP (200 ML) MILK
2 EGGS
4 TBSP (50 G) CANE SUGAR
1 ORGANIC LEMON (OR ORGANIC ORANGE)
PINCH OF CINNAMON
4–6 SLICES DAY-OLD WHITE BREAD
2 TBSP BUTTER

To make the French toast, beat together the milk, eggs, and 1 tablespoon of the sugar. Wash the lemon in hot water and zest it. In a deep plate, stir together the zest, the remaining sugar, and a pinch of cinnamon. Dip the bread in the egg mixture. Heat the butter in a non-stick skillet until it foams. Fry the bread slices on both sides until golden brown. Lightly dip the bread into the sugar mixture. Serve with the vanilla sauce.

★ *Deluxe* ★ *Slow food* ★ *Festive*

Plum and marzipan dumplings

SERVES 4

1 LB 2 OZ (500 G) STARCHY POTATOES, SUCH AS RUSSET

5 ½ OZ (150 G) BREAD FLOUR

½ CUP PLUS 1 TBSP (125 G) BUTTER

1 TBSP SEMOLINA FLOUR

1 EGG

PINCH OF SALT

1 CUP (100 G) BREADCRUMBS

1 LB 2 OZ (500 G) RIPE PLUMS

7 OZ (200 G) MARZIPAN

1 TBSP SUGAR AND 1 TSP SALT, FOR THE COOKING WATER

1 TSP POWDERED SUGAR

Bring all ingredients to room temperature. This is especially important for the butter and the eggs.

Boil the potatoes in salted water for 20 minutes, or until tender. Drain, peel, and mash the potatoes. Let the steam evaporate. Place the potatoes in a bowl. Add the flour, 3 tablespoons (40 g) of the butter, the semolina, egg, and salt. Knead to make a dough. Heat the remaining butter in a frying pan until it foams. Add the breadcrumbs and fry until golden brown. Wash the plums and remove the pits, keeping the plums whole. Cut the marzipan into small pieces and place a piece inside each plum.

Shape the dough into a thick log. Cut the dough into slices and place a filled plum on top of each slice. Moisten your hands with water and shape the slices into dumplings, sealing the edges well so that the plums stay covered.

In a large pot, bring plenty of water to a boil. Add the salt and sugar. Place the dumplings in the water and reduce heat to a bare simmer. Cook the dumplings until they rise to the surface and turn over. Remove dumplings from the water with a slotted spoon, roll to coat with toasted breadcrumbs, and dust with powdered sugar.

WINTRY DESSERTS

THESE YUMMY "TORN" PANCAKES ARE A TRUE WINTER TREAT. IDEALLY SERVED STRAIGHT OUT
OF A LARGE, HOT CAST-IRON SKILLET, THEY ARE PERFECT WITH A FRUITY APPLE, PEAR,
OR SOUR CHERRY COMPOTE, OR WITH CARAMELIZED PLUMS OR CRANBERRIES, OR ICE CREAM.

SERVES 2

CARAMELIZED
Polenta pancakes

2 CUPS (500 ML) MILK   5 ½ OZ (150 G) POLENTA (CORNMEAL)
2 – 3 EGGS   2 TBSP BUTTER   2 – 4 TBSP SLIVERED ALMONDS   2 – 4 TBSP RUM RAISINS (SEE TIP)
ZEST OF ½ ORGANIC LEMON   3 TBSP CANE SUGAR   PINCH OF SALT
1 – 2 TBSP CLARIFIED BUTTER, FOR BAKING   1 TBSP POWDERED SUGAR, FOR DUSTING

Place the milk in a saucepan and bring to a boil. Stirring constantly, slowly add the polenta to the saucepan. Reduce the heat. Still stirring, let the polenta soak up the liquid for about 5 minutes. Let cool slightly.

Separate the eggs. Working quickly, whisk the egg yolks, 1 tablespoon of butter, the almonds, raisins, and lemon zest into the polenta mixture.

Beat the egg whites with a pinch of salt in a bowl until stiff peaks form. As you are finishing, beat in 1 table-spoon of sugar. You can use a spoon, a whisk, or an electric hand mixer for this step. Fold the egg whites into the polenta mixture.

Melt the clarified butter in a frying pan over a low heat. Add the polenta mixture and smooth the top to make a pancake. When it is golden brown underneath, divide the pancake into 4. It doesn't matter if the batter on top has not quite set. Flip the pieces and fry the other side until golden brown.

And now, the grand finale: using 2 cooking spoons, tear the quarters into bite-sized pieces. Add the remaining tablespoon of butter and 2 tablespoons of sugar. Cook the pancake pieces over medium high until caramelized. Dust sparingly with powdered sugar before serving.

Do try an apple or pear version, too: simply stir thinly sliced apples or pears into the polenta mixture.

TIP

You can buy rum-soaked raisins, of course, but try making them yourself. It is quick and easy, and the raisins don't need to be soaked for very long. To make rum raisins, place 4 tablespoons raisins, 2 tablespoons rum, and 4 tablespoons water in a saucepan. Bring to a boil, remove from heat, and let swell briefly. Now they are ready to use. They taste a great deal better than pack-aged rum raisins, which tend to be very hard.

241

WINTRY DESSERTS

Holler
Punsch

HOT DRINKS

WHETHER YOU MAKE THESE DRINKS AT
HOME OR IN THE MOUNTAINS, SERVE THEM WARM
IN WINTER. WHEN IT IS BITTERLY COLD OUTSIDE
AND YOU NEED COMFORTING WARMTH
FROM THE INSIDE, SPIKE THEM WITH SOME ALCOHOL.
OF COURSE, THEY ARE ALSO GREAT FOR TAKING ALONG
WITH YOU ON A SKIING TOUR IN A THERMOS.

Poacher's tea

WHETHER POACHER OR HUNTER, THIS HOT
ALCOHOLIC DRINK REVIVES EVERYONE!
ACCORDING TO LOCAL LORE, LUMBERJACKS AND
HUNTERS IN THE TYROLEAN FORESTS DRANK
THIS TEA AS A TONIC. IF YOU PLAN ON TAKING IT
ALONG WITH YOU IN THE BACKCOUNTRY, LEAVE
OUT THE SCHNAPPS; THE SWEET TEA WILL
WARM AND FORTIFY YOU ENOUGH ON ITS OWN!

CARAMELIZED
Poacher's tea

MAKES 4 MUGS OR FILLS 1 THERMOS

1 ¾ CUPS (400 ML) FRESHLY BREWED BLACK TEA
¾ CUP (200 ML) RED WINE
¾ CUP (200 ML) ORANGE JUICE (IDEALLY FRESH)
2 TBSP CANE SUGAR
4 ORANGE SLICES
1 CINNAMON STICK
2 WHOLE CLOVES
2 SHOTS (¾ FL OZ/20 ML) FRUIT SCHNAPPS
OR RUM (OPTIONAL)

Make the black tea separately; steep it for about 3 minutes.
Heat the remaining ingredients in a saucepan, then add the tea
and the fruit schnapps or rum, if using. Remove the spices.
Instead of the cane sugar, you could also soak a sugar cube with
the schnapps, place it on a spoon and set it alight briefly.
This decreases the effects of the alcohol and intensifies the flavor.

ALCOHOL-FREE VERSION

Replace the red wine with red grape juice, and, of course, leave out
the schnapps. You can add a few drops of rum extract instead.

HOMEMADE
Fire starters

IT'S A COLD WINTER EVENING. ICE CRYSTALS ARE BUILDING ON THE WINDOWS, THE FIRE IS CRACKLING IN THE FIREPLACE, AND YOU ARE SAVORING A STEAMING MUG OF HOT CHOCOLATE IN FRONT OF THE FIRE. BUT, BEFORE YOU GET TO THAT POINT, THE FIRE HAS TO BE COAXED INTO LIFE IN THE FIREPLACE. THIS IS A SIMPLE TASK USING HOMEMADE FIRE STARTERS. THEY ARE QUICK AND EASY TO MAKE FROM AN EGG CARTON, WOOD SHAVINGS, AND A BIT OF WAX. IN FACT, NATURE PROVIDES MANY MATERIALS THAT ARE EXCELLENT FOR BUILDING A BLAZING FIRE. JUST MAKE SURE ALL THE MATERIALS ARE COMPLETELY DRY. OF COURSE, YOU CAN ALSO USE THESE FIRE STARTERS MADE OF RECYCLED MATERIALS TO START A CHARCOAL BARBECUE.

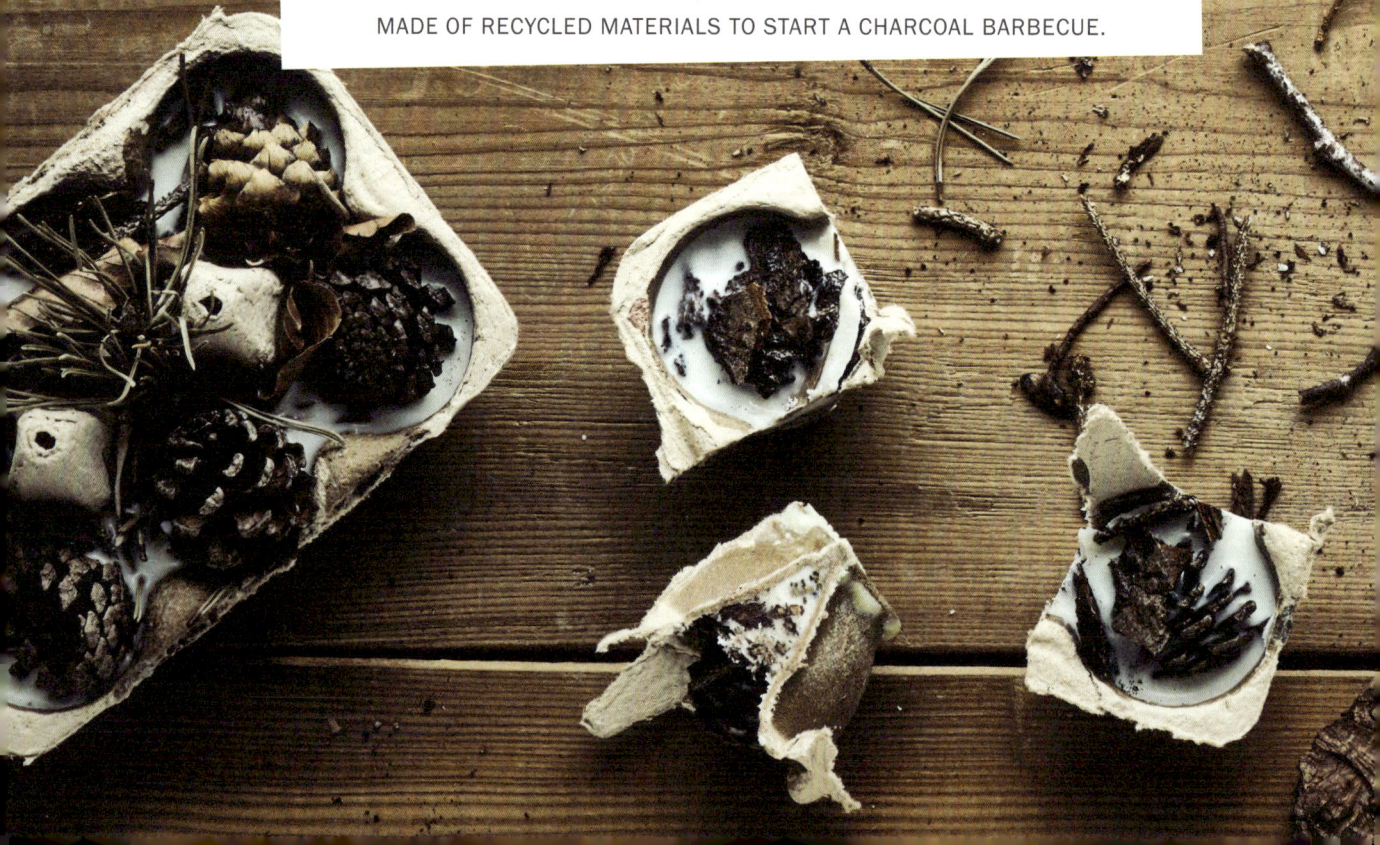

THE FOLLOWING MATERIALS ARE ESPECIALLY WELL-SUITED TO MAKING FIRE STARTERS:

- small dry pine cones
- small pieces of dry sticks and twigs, for kindling
- wood shavings, sawdust
- softwood shavings (excelsior) or cardboard strips (both are packing material)

YOU WILL ALSO NEED:

- wax candle stubs
- egg cartons or toilet roll cardboard tubes

To make this small energy bundle from wood, cardboard, and wax, simply fill an egg carton or toilet roll cardboard tube with the dry wood shavings and kindling, and place small pinecones in the middle. Slowly melt the wax in an old saucepan. Pour the liquid wax over the dry materials in the egg carton or in the toilet roll tube. If you are using the latter, place it on a piece of cardboard first. Let harden overnight. Break the egg carton or cut the toilet roll tube into individual pieces. Homemade fire starters are a sustainable alternative to the store-bought, commercial ones.

MAKES 4 MUGS OR FILLS 1 THERMOS

Hot ginger and lemon tea

THIS AMAZING SPICY DRINK IS A REAL IMMUNE BOOSTER. AT THE FIRST SLIGHT SIGN OF A COLD, YOU CAN OFTEN STOP IT IN ITS TRACKS BY DRINKING COPIOUS AMOUNTS OF HOT GINGER AND LEMON TEA. GINGER HAS AN ANTIBACTERIAL EFFECT; THE VITAMIN C IN THE LEMON HELPS STRENGTHEN YOUR IMMUNE SYSTEM; THE PIPERINE CONTAINED IN BLACK PEPPER BOOSTS THE HEALTH-PROMOTING EFFECTS OF THE CURCUMIN CONTAINED IN TURMERIC; AND HONEY CALMS AND COMFORTS THE THROAT.

BUT THE MOST IMPORTANT THING?
IT TASTES DELICIOUS!

2 1-IN (2 ½ CM) PIECES OF GINGER
3 CUPS (750 ML) WATER
JUICE OF 1 ORGANIC LEMON
½ TSP GROUND TURMERIC
PINCH OF CINNAMON
PINCH OF BLACK PEPPER
1 – 2 TBSP HONEY

Peel the ginger, grate or very finely mince it, and place it in a saucepan. Add the water and bring to a boil. Simmer for 10 minutes. Strain the mixture through a sieve and return it to the saucepan. Add the lemon juice. Reheat the ginger potion briefly, but don't let it boil. Add the spices and sweeten to taste with honey.

WE KEEP A FEW HAPPY CHICKENS ON OUR PROPERTY,
SO WE ALWAYS HAVE FRESH, ORGANIC EGGS ON HAND. TO MAKE THE BEST
OF THEM IN AN ESPECIALLY APPETIZING WAY, WE MAKE
A FEW BOTTLES OF EGG LIQUEUR FOR THE WINTER. HOMEMADE EGG
LIQUEUR MAKES EGG PUNCH TASTE EXTRAORDINARILY GOOD. DO YOU KNOW
AND LIKE BOMBARDINOS, THE EGG LIQUEUR-BASED ALCOHOLIC
DRINK POPULAR IN ALPINE SKI AREAS? IF SO, THIS IS JUST THE RIGHT
RECIPE FOR YOUR NEXT APRÈS-SKI!

MAKES 4 MUGS OR FILLS 1 THERMOS

Egg punch

1 ¾ CUPS (400 ML) MILK   1 CINNAMON STICK
1 CUP (200 G) HEAVY CREAM
¾ CUP (200 ML) HOMEMADE EGG LIQUEUR (PAGE 42) OR
STORE-BOUGHT EGG LIQUEUR
3 TBSP AMARETTO OR RUM   PINCH OF CINNAMON

In a saucepan, bring the milk and the cinnamon stick
to a boil. In a bowl, combine half of the cream with
the egg liqueur and the amaretto or rum. Add this mixture
to the hot milk, but don't let it boil any further! Remove
the cinnamon stick. Ladle the egg punch into glasses.
Whip the remaining cream until soft peaks form. Divide
the whipped cream among the glasses and sprinkle
ground cinnamon on top.

★ *Quick* ★ *Warming* ★ *Winter picnic*

MULLED WINE IS A TRUE WINTER CLASSIC; ONE THAT TASTES
ESPECIALLY GOOD WHEN YOU MAKE IT YOURSELF. USE
A DRY, ROBUST RED WINE—YOU'LL WANT A WINE THAT STANDS UP
TO THE HIGHLY FLAVORED SPICES. SWEET WINES ARE LESS WELL-SUITED,
SINCE IT IS HARDER TO REGULATE THE AMOUNT OF SUGAR.

Classic mulled red wine

MAKES 4 MUGS OR FILLS 1 THERMOS

1 ORGANIC ORANGE
1 BOTTLE (750 ML) ORGANIC DRY RED WINE (SUCH AS PINOT NOIR)
ZEST OF 1 ORGANIC LEMON
2–3 TBSP CANE SUGAR, GRANULATED SUGAR, HONEY, OR AGAVE SYRUP
2 TBSP MULLED WINE SPICES (PAGE 39)
OPTIONAL: SEEDS OF ½ VANILLA BEAN

Wash the orange in hot water and cut it into thin slices. In a saucepan, add the wine, lemon zest, and sugar, honey, or agave syrup. Put the mulled wine spices in a tea ball infuser and place it in the liquid. Heat the mixture to 165 °F (75 °C). Cover the saucepan, turn off the heat, and let steep for at least 30 minutes. Strain the mulled wine through a fine-mesh sieve. Add the seeds of the vanilla bean, if using. Taste and adjust for sweetness. Return wine to the saucepan, reheat, and serve.

TIP

To ensure your mulled wine stays hot for longer in the thermos, rinse your thermos with hot water before filling it with wine. Then head outside to the campfire!

HOT DRINKS

Punch

Hot punch and bitterly cold winter evenings go hand-in-hand.
Take your favorite punch outdoors with you in an insulated mug.
Standing by the firebowl in front of the hut, it will warm you from the inside out!

HOT BLOOD ORANGE PUNCH

6 BLOOD ORANGES   1 LIME   1 IN (2 ½ CM) PIECE OF GINGER
1 STAR ANISE   1 STALK LEMONGRASS, CUT IN HALF   2 TBSP HONEY

Juice 5 of the oranges and the lime. You should end up with 1 ¾–2 cups/400–500 ml of juice. Place the juice in a saucepan. Peel and mince the ginger, then add it to the saucepan along with the star anise and the lemongrass. Heat the mixture slowly, but don't let it boil! Stir in the honey. Cut the remaining orange in half, then into slices. Place 2–3 slices in each glass. Ladle punch into the glasses and serve immediately.

TIP

For an alcoholic version, add ¾ fl oz (2 cl) orange liqueur to each serving.

HOT BLACKCURRANT PUNCH

1 ¾ CUPS (400 ML) ORGANIC BLACKCURRANT JUICE   1 ¾ CUPS (400 ML) RED WINE
½–⅔ CUP (100–150 ML) HOMEMADE BLACKCURRANT LIQUEUR (PAGE 43), OR STORE-BOUGHT
2 STAR ANISE   1–2 CINNAMON STICKS   3–4 TBSP BROWN CANE SUGAR   1 STAR FRUIT

Place the blackcurrant juice in a saucepan. Add the wine, blackcurrant liqueur, star anise, cinnamon sticks, and sugar. Stir and slowly heat to 165 °F (75 °C). Cover the saucepan, turn off the heat, and let steep for 20 minutes. Wash and slice the star fruit. Divide the fruit among glasses, and ladle hot punch into each glass.

HOT ELDERBERRY PUNCH

1 ¾ CUPS (400 ML) ELDERBERRY JUICE (HOMEMADE OR STORE-BOUGHT)   ¾ CUP (200 ML) GRAPE JUICE
JUICE OF 1 LEMON   ¾ CUP (200 ML) FRESHLY BREWED RED FRUIT TEA
2 TBSP BROWN SUGAR   1 CINNAMON STICK   HANDFUL OF DRIED CHERRIES
***OPTIONAL:** 1 DASH RUM AND/OR 1 PINCH CHILI POWDER*

Heat the elderberry juice, grape juice, and lemon juice in a saucepan, but do not boil. Add the tea, sugar, cinnamon stick, and dried cherries. Let steep for 5 minutes. For a more fiery version, add a dash of rum and a pinch of chili powder.

MAKES 4–5 MUGS OF EACH KIND

Hot chocolate

It's a well-known fact that chocolate improves the mood and brings happiness!
But it has other positive qualities, too: for example, high-quality
dark chocolate lowers blood pressure. For the very best taste (and to enjoy
it in good conscience), I urge you to purchase only fair trade,
high-quality organic chocolate. Each of the three recipes that
follow makes a different kind of chocolate lollipop
which is then used in hot chocolate. The lollipops will slide out easily
if you use straight round shot glasses, or glasses that are
narrower at the bottom than at the top.

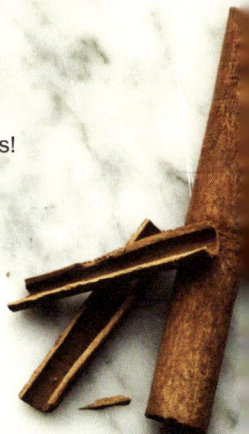

NOUGAT HOT CHOCOLATE

3 ½ OZ (100 G) DARK CHOCOLATE COUVERTURE (AT LEAST 70% COCOA)
1 ¾ OZ (50 G) NOUGAT
ZEST OF ½ ORGANIC ORANGE

YOU WILL ALSO NEED:
4 – 5 SHOT GLASSES
4 – 5 WOODEN STICKS OR SMALL WOODEN SPOONS

Melt the chocolate over a water bath over very low heat,
stirring constantly. Add half of the nougat and melt it, too.
Stir in the zest. Cut the remaining nougat into small cubes.

Divide the chocolate mixture among the glasses. Sprinkle with the nougat pieces.
When the chocolate begins to harden, place a wooden stick or wooden
spoon into each glass to make a lollipop. Let harden overnight in the refrigerator.
Remove the lollipops from the glasses. If needed, dip them briefly in warm water
to loosen from the glasses.

259

CARAMEL HOT CHOCOLATE

5 ½ OZ (150 G) MILK CHOCOLATE COUVERTURE
PINCH OF CINNAMON AND GROUND CARDAMOM
4 CARAMELS (PAGE 130), CHOPPED INTO SMALL PIECES

YOU WILL ALSO NEED:
4–5 SHOT GLASSES   4–5 WOODEN STICKS OR SMALL WOODEN SPOONS

Melt the chocolate over a water bath set over low heat, stirring constantly.
Stir in the spices. Divide the chocolate mixture among the glasses.
Sprinkle with the chopped caramels. When the chocolate begins to harden,
place a wooden stick or wooden spoon into each glass.
Let harden overnight in the refrigerator. Remove the lollipops from the glasses.
If needed, dip them briefly in warm water to loosen from the glasses.

WHITE HOT CHOCOLATE WITH TUMERIC

5 ½ OZ (150 G) WHITE CHOCOLATE COUVERTURE   PINCH OF CINNAMON
PINCH OF GROUND ALLSPICE   PINCH OF TURMERIC   SEEDS OF ½ VANILLA BEAN

YOU WILL ALSO NEED:
4–5 SHOT GLASSES   4–5 WOODEN STICKS OR SMALL WOODEN SPOONS

Slowly melt the chocolate over a water bath, stirring constantly.
Stir in the spices and the vanilla seeds. Divide the chocolate mixture among
the glasses. When the chocolate begins to harden, place a wooden stick or wooden
spoon into each glass. Let harden overnight in the refrigerator.
Remove the lollipops from the glasses. If needed, dip them briefly
in warm water to loosen from the glasses.

FOR DRINKING: In a saucepan, bring 1 cup of milk per serving to a boil.
Place 1 lollipop in each mug and pour in the hot milk. After 2 minutes,
or when the chocolate has melted completely, stir with the lollipop stick or spoon.

FOR THE ROAD: Pour 1 cup of hot milk per serving into a thermos.
Wrap the chocolate lollipops in waxed paper and stick them in your backpack.
Now and then I like to eat the chocolate lollipops on their own, without the milk.

HOT DRINKS

I FIRST DRANK THIS DELICIOUS, FLAVORFUL HOT MILK ON A DIVING TRIP TO EGYPT. IT IS LOCALLY KNOWN AS *SAHLEB*, AND IT'S A VERY POPULAR CAFÉ DRINK. EGYPTIANS OFTEN ADD A DASH OF ROSEWATER OR ORANGE OIL, BUT THESE MAKE THE DRINK TASTE TOO PERFUMED FOR MY TASTE, SO I CHOOSE NOT TO ADD EITHER. WITH ITS CINNAMON TASTE AND ITS COMFORTING WARMTH, SAHLEB IS WONDERFUL FOR OUR WINTERS, TOO.

★ *Quick* ★ *Warming*

Hot cinnamon milk

1 HEAPING TSP CORNSTARCH   2 CUPS (500 ML) MILK
CANE SUGAR OR HONEY, TO TASTE   PINCH OF CINNAMON
2 TSP FINELY CHOPPED, UNSALTED SHELLED PISTACHIOS

Place the cornstarch and a small amount of the milk in a cup.
Stir until smooth. Place the remaining milk in a small saucepan, and sweeten to taste with sugar or honey.
Bring to a boil, then reduce the heat to medium. Add the cornstarch, stirring constantly.
Simmer until the milk has thickened. Ladle the milk into mugs. Sprinkle each serving with
a pinch of cinnamon and chopped pistachios.

★ *Warming* ★ *Deluxe* ★ *Festive*

Festive gingerbread latte

1 ¾ CUPS (400 ML) MILK
GERMAN GINGERBREAD SPICE MIX:
PINCH OF GROUND CINNAMON, GROUND GINGER, GROUND ALLSPICE
1 CARDAMOM POD   2 WHOLE CLOVES
2 TSP HONEY   2 CUPS BREWED HOT ESPRESSO OR STRONG COFFEE
½ CUP (100 G) HEAVY CREAM, WHIPPED
2 TBSP GRATED DARK CHOCOLATE

Heat the milk, gingerbread spices, and honey in a small saucepan. Remove the cardamom and cloves.
Place the espresso in a cup or glass and pour in the spiced milk.
Spoon the whipped cream on top, and garnish with a pinch of cinnamon and grated chocolate.

YOU
CAN'T
GIVE
YOUR
LIFE
MORE
TIME,
SO
GIVE
THE
TIME
YOU
HAVE
LEFT
MORE
LIFE.

SPECIAL THANKS

Another year has gone by and I am happy to send my second book along with you on your travels. This time the book took us to far-flung corners in the mountains, to wonderful countries, to magical winter landscapes. Bravely, my **PHOTOGRAPHY TEAM** accompanied me through the deep snow in the woods of the Caucasus in Georgia, to the northern edge of Europe, to the Lofoten Islands in Norway, and to the snowy Tyrolean mountain landscape.

Thanks to **MAJOLA** for all the close and personal work together over many years, and for your active sponsorship.

To **TINA** and **ANGELA** of Umschau-Verlag, a big thank you. Thanks for your support and for never losing sight of the big picture.

ANNE FISCHER for every shared moment and for the many that are yet to come. The next adventure already awaits us. Thank you for taking care of our sponsor and for all your marketing work.

To **ANTJE** and **RIKE** from Wildhood-Store (www.wildhood store.de), **ORTOVOX** (www.ortovox.com), and **THERMOS** (www.thermos.com), for equipping us with innovative and beautiful props for our photo shoots. My buddies **DIGGER** and **AKKI** from the **WHITEHEARTS SKI CREW** (www. whitehearts.de) for the unforgettable time together in the depths of the Georgian Caucasus. Many thanks for the action photos on pages 6–7, 58–59, 76–77, 168–169, 186–187, 195, 234–235 to **DIRK WAGENER** (aka Digger).

To our models, friends, and hardworking helpers: **JACOBA KRIECHMAYR**; **KATHI** and **PAUL** from the **VAN NOMADEN**; **DAV DIESSEN**; **ANNE**; **VERA**; **BIANCA** and **MICHI**; as well as our **NORDIC WALKING SKI CREW**.

WWW.THE-GREAT-OUTDOORS.DE
INSTAGRAM: THEGREATOUTDOORSBOOK

INGREDIENTS INDEX

MINT

Pea Soup with Egg and Sausage 91

MUSHROOMS

Barley Risotto 148

Dried Wild Mushrooms 18

MUSTARD

Lamb's Lettuce with Bacon 142

Roast Pork 183

South Tyrolean Dumpling Salad 161

NOUGAT

Nougat Hot Chocolate 258

OATS

Fruity Fitness Porridge 50

Original Swiss Bircher Muesli 53

Spiced Porridge 50

ONION

Alpine Breakfast Hash 72

Barley Risotto 148

Barley Stew 102

Basic Bread Dumplings 214

Beef Stock 188

Bread Dumplings with Alpine Cheese 210

Bread Soup with Beer 98

Carrot Soup with Ginger and Honey 82

Chicken Stew 84

Chicken Tagine with Preserved Lemon 162

Chunky Potato Stew 87

Cream of Squash Soup 88

Creamed Cabbage 194

Crepe Soup 100

Pea Soup with Egg and Sausage 91

Hearty Goulash 187

Homemade Pickled Herring 26

Homemade Blaukraut (Braised Red Cabbage) 29

Horseradish Soup 83

Lamb's Lettuce with Bacon 142

One-Pot Chicken Pasta 152

One-Pot Tagliatelle 156

Pan-Fried Fish Fillets 145

Pasta with Wild Game Ragú 198

Pickled Herring in Creamy Sauce 151

Poached Beef with Root Vegetables 193

Potato Noodles with Sauerkraut 208

Potato Pancakes 75

Pretzel Casserole 216

Red Curry Paste 23

Roast Pork 183

Spinach Spätzle 202

Swabian Ravioli 212

Sweet Potato Frittata with Kale 56

Sweet Potato Soup with Fresh Chilies 92

Tyrolean Hash 194

Warming Winter Curry 170

Wild Game Burger 177

Wintry Roasted Vegetables 138

Zucchini Chutney 30

ORANGE JUICE

Caramelized Poacher's Tea 248

Winter Salad 141

PAPRIKA

Chicken Stew 84

Chicken Tagine with Preserved Lemon 162

PARMESAN CHEESE

Barley Risotto 148

Gnocchi 146

One-Pot Chicken Pasta 152

Pizzoccheri 201

South Tyrolean Dumpling Salad 161

Swabian Ravioli 212

PARSLEY

Alpine Breakfast Hash 72

Barley Risotto 148

Barley Stew 102

Beef Stock 188

Bread Dumplings with

Alpine Cheese 210

Bread Soup with Beer 98

Carrot Soup with Ginger and Honey 82

Chicken Stew 84

Chunky Potato Stew 87

Cream of Squash Soup 88

Crepe Soup 100

Pea Soup with Egg and Sausage 91

Gnocchi 146

Hearty Goulash 187

Herbed Crepes 106

One-Pot Chicken Pasta 152

Pan-Fried Fish Fillets 145

Pasta with Wild Game Ragú 198

Pretzel Casserole 216

Swabian Ravioli 212

Tyrolean Hash 194

PARSNIP

Horseradish Soup 83

PASTA

One-Pot Penne with Chicken 152

One-Pot Tagliatelle 156

PEAR

Fruity Fitness Porridge 50

Winter Smoothie, Santa's Hat 71

Winter Smoothie, Hot Stag 71

PEANUTS

Peanut Butter 21

PEAS

Barley Stew 102

Pea Soup with Egg and Sausage 91

PECANS

Autumn Storm Winter Trail Mix 113

Fruity Fitness Porridge 50

Mini Chocolate Brownies 114

PINE NUTS

Autumn Storm Winter Trail Mix 113

Hot Cinnamon Milk 260

PISTACHIOS

Sweet Potato Frittata with Kale 56

PLUMS

Homemade Liqueurs 41

Plum and Marzipan Dumplings 239

POLENTA

Caramelized Polenta Pancakes 240

POMEGRANATE

Fruity Fitness Porridge 50

POTATO

Alpine Breakfast Hash 72

Barley Stew 102

Chicken Stew 84

Chicken Tagine with Preserved Lemon 162

Chunky Potato Stew 87

Gnocchi 146

Horseradish Soup 83

Pickled Herring in Creamy Sauce 151

Pizzoccheri 201

Plum and Marzipan Dumplings 239

Poached Beef with Root Vegetables 193

Potato Doughnuts 211

Potato Noodles with Sauerkraut 208

Potato Pancakes with Smoked Salmon 75

Potato and Celery Root Purée 204

Tyrolean Hash 194

Wedges 197

Wintry Roasted Vegetables 138

PUMPKIN SEEDS

Autumn Storm Winter Trail Mix 113

Gnocchi with Squash 146

PORK

Barley Stew 102

Roast Pork 183

QUARK CHEESE

Fresh Cheese Crepes Baked in Custard 228

Fresh Cheese Dumplings 222

Potato Doughnuts 211

RADICCHIO

South Tyrolean Dumpling Salad 161

Winter Salad 141

RAISINS

Apple Strudel 226

Caramelized Polenta Pancakes 240

Fruit Bars 118

Original Swiss Bircher Muesli 53

Spiced Porridge 50

Zucchini Chutney 30

RED BEET

Red Beet Dumplings 215

Red Beet Semolina Dumplings 105

Warm Red Beet Salad 159

Winter Smoothie, Santa's Hat 71

Wintry Roasted Vegetables 138

RED CABBAGE

Homemade Blaukraut

(Braised Red Cabbage) 29

Red Cabbage Salad 166

RED CHILI PEPPER

Carrot Soup with Ginger and Honey 82

Chicken Stew 84

Chicken Tagine with Preserved Lemon 162

Cream of Squash Soup 88

Gnocchi 146

Red Curry Paste 23

Sweet Potato Soup with Fresh Chilies 92

RED WINE

Blackcurrant Punch 257

Caramelized Poacher's Tea 248

Homemade Blaukraut (Braised Red Cabbage) 29

Pasta with Wild Game Ragú 198

Venison Medallions 204

RICE

Warming Winter Curry 170

RICOTTA

Fresh Cheese Crepes Baked in Custard 228

Fresh Cheese Dumplings 222

Gnocchi 146

Potato Doughnuts 211

RUM

Blackcurrant Liqueur 43

Caramelized Poacher's Tea 248

Caramelized Polenta Pancakes 240

Egg Liqueur 42

Egg Punch 254

Fresh Cheese Crepes Baked in Custard 228

Hot Elderberry Punch 257

Plum Liqueur 41

SAUERKRAUT

Potato Noodles with Sauerkraut 208

Szegedine Goulash 195

SAUSAGE, WURST

Pea Soup with Egg and Sausage 91

SAVOY CABBAGE

Pizzoccheri 201

Creamed Cabbage 194

SEMOLINA

Plum and Marzipan Dumplings 239

Red Beet Semolina Dumplings 105

SHALLOTS

Barley Risotto 148

Chicken Stew 84

Chunky Potato Stew 87

Creamed Cabbage 194

Egg and Ham Toast Cups 54

Gnocchi 146

HAM

Pan-Fried fish Fillets 145

Poached Beef with Root Vegetables 193

Swabian Ravioli 212

Wintry Roasted Vegetables 138

SHRIMP

Shrimp Paste 23

SMOKED SALMON

Egg and Ham Toast Cups 54

One-Pot Tagliatelle 156

Potato Pancakes with Smoked Salmon 75

SOUR CREAM

Blueberry Pancakes 75

Bread Dumplings with Alpine Cheese 210

Chunky Potato Stew 87

Fresh Cheese Crepes Baked in Custard 228

Fresh Cheese Dumplings 222

One-Pot Tagliatelle 156

Pickled Herring in Creamy Sauce 151

Potato Doughnuts 211

Potato Pancakes with Smoked Salmon 75

Sweet Potato Soup with Fresh Chilies 92

Szegedine Goulash 195

Warm Red Beet Salad 159

Winter Smoothie, Santa's Hat 71

SOY SAUCE

One-Pot Penne with Chicken 152

Warming Winter Curry 170

SPINACH

One-Pot Tagliatelle with Smoked Salmon 156

Spinach and Cheese Dumplings 215

Spinach Spätzle 202

SQUASH

Cream of Squash Soup 88

Gnocchi 146

Toasted Pumpkin Seeds 107

Warming Winter Curry 170

Wintry Roasted Vegetables 138

STAR FRUIT

Blackcurrant Punch 257

SWEET POTATO

Potato Pancakes with Smoked Salmon 75

Sweet Potato Frittata with Kale 56

Sweet Potato Wedges 177

Sweet Potato Soup with Fresh Chilies 92

Warming Winter Curry 170

Wintry Roasted Vegetables 138

THAI CHILI

Red Curry Paste 23

TOMATO

Alpine Breakfast Hash 72

Baked Avocados 56

Bread Soup with Beer 98

Chicken Stew 84

Chicken Tagine with Preserved Lemon 162

One-Pot Chicken Pasta 152

Pasta with Wild Game Ragú 198

Wild Game Burger 177

TONKA BEAN

Egg Liqueur 42

VANILLA BEAN

Blackcurrant Liqueur 43

Caramel Hot Chocolate 259

Caramels 130

Egg Liqueur 42

French Toast with Vanilla Sauce 238

Fresh Cheese Crepes Baked in Custard 228

Fresh Cheese Dumplings 222

Mini Chocolate Brownies 114

VANILLA SUGAR

Blueberry Pancakes 75

Candied Almonds 121

Homemade Vanilla Sugar 43

Spekulatius Spice Cookies 36

Stollen Balls 35

Vanilla Crescent Cookies 36

VEAL, GROUND

Crepe Soup 100

Swabian Ravioli 212

VEGETABLE STOCK

Barley Risotto 148

Barley Stew 102

Bread Soup with Beer 98

Carrot Soup with Ginger and Honey 82

Chicken Stew 84

Chunky Potato Stew 87

Cream of Squash Soup 88

Crepe Soup 100

Pea Soup with Egg and Sausage 91

Hearty Goulash 187

Horseradish Soup 83

One-Pot Tagliatelle 156

Pan-Fried Fish Fillets 145

Pasta with Wild Game Ragú 198

Poached Beef with Root Vegetables 193

Sweet Potato Soup with Fresh Chilies 92

WALNUTS

Apple Strudel 226

Autumn Storm Winter Trail Mix 113

Carrot Cake Balls 114

Cold-Proofed Buns 68

Dukkah 22

Mini Chocolate Brownies 114

Potato Pancakes with Smoked Salmon 75

Pretzel Casserole 216

Red Beet Semolina Dumplings 105

Red Cabbage Salad 166

Spiced Porridge 50

Spinach Spätzle 202

Vanilla Crescent Cookies 36

Warm Red Beet Salad 159

Winter Salad 141

Winter Smoothie, Santa's Hat 71

WHITE WINE

Barley Risotto 148

Chicken Stew 84

Cream of Squash Soup 88

Gnocchi 146

Horseradish Soup 83

YEAST

Cold-Proofed Buns 68

Crusty Farmer's Bread 60

Fluffy Yeast Dumplings 225

Paillasse-style Bread 69

Pita Bread with Sesame and Nigella 67

Stollen Balls 35

Yellow Burger Buns 176

YOGURT

Pea Soup with Egg and Sausage 91

Pickled Herring in Creamy Sauce 151

Potato Pancakes with Smoked Salmon 75

Winter Smoothie, Old Swede 71

ZUCCHINI

Chicken Stew 84

Egg and Ham Toast Cups 54

Zucchini Chutney 30

RECIPE INDEX

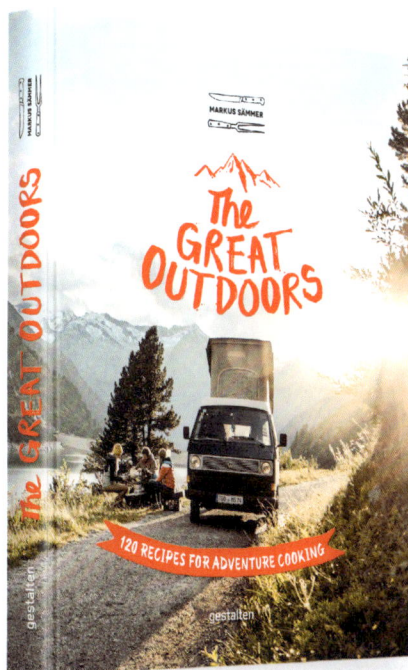

... and for your
summer adventures

THE GREAT OUTDOORS

120 RECIPES FOR
ADVENTURE COOKING

ISBN: 978-3-89955-948-4

IMPRINT

RECIPES, TEXT, IDEA

Markus Sämmer, markus-saemmer.de
instagram.com/thegreatoutdoorsbook

TRANSLATION

Barbara Hopkinson

COPY-EDITING

Katie Roussos

PROJECT MANAGEMENT

Lars Pietzschmann

PHOTOGRAPHY LIFESTYLE, OUTDOOR & SPORT

Steffen Schulte Lippern, Studio-Steve.de

LAYOUT, ILLUSTRATION

Katharina Lanz, www.vannomaden.de

LAYOUT AND ART DIRECTION

Tina Defaux, www.umschau-verlag.de

FOOD PHOTOGRAPHY

Julia Ruby Hildebrand, Ingolf Hatz
Photographers BFF, www.augustundjuli.de

TYPEFACES

Brandon Printed Extras by Hannes von Döhren,
Franklin Gothic by Morris Fuller Benton,
Outfitter Script by Gilang Purnama Jaya,
Renovation by Veneta Rangelova, True North
Textures by Cindy Kinash and Charles Gibbons

EDITED by Robert Klanten

PRINTED by Nino Druck GmbH,

Neustadt/Weinstraße
Made in Germany

PUBLISHED by gestalten, Berlin 2019

ISBN 978-3-89955-650-6

The German original edition THE GREAT OUTDOORS—WINTER COOKING
was published 2017 by Neuer Umschau Buchverlag GmbH,
Im Altenschemel 21, 67435 Neustadt/Weinstraße, Germany.

© for the English edition: Die Gestalten Verlag GmbH & Co. KG, Berlin 2019.

For more information, and to order books, please visit www.gestalten.com.

Bibliographic information published by the Deutsche Nationalbibliothek.
The Deutsche Nationalbibliothek lists this publication in the Deutsche
Nationalbibliografie; detailed bibliographic data are available online at www.dnb.de.

This book was printed on paper certified according to the standards of the FSC®.

MIX
Paper from
responsible sources
FSC
www.fsc.org
FSC® C006655